Dedicated to my parents, wife and kids -
my constant support and
a huge motivating force in life

PRAISE AND APPRECIATION FOR ORIGINAL EDITION

The original edition received multiple 5-star reviews on Amazon and wonderful comments from readers. Here are some comments and appreciation received so far that highlight all the value readers have received from reading the book.

The author uses language that is easily understood and relatable in business as well as everyday situations which, in my opinion, makes it a unique, enjoyable learning opportunity for anyone who is interested in improving their negotiation skills - for either business or personal use. The book makes the reader realize how often we tend to actually use our negotiation muscle, either consciously or sub-consciously every single day.
-**A senior program manager, SF Bay Area**

The book does an amazing job at breaking down everything there is about negotiating, from the psychology to the benefits. I can honestly say that most of the material in the book was refreshing and informative. The book is written in short, punchy, content-rich chapters, each page is filled with actionable strategies and tactics.
-**A finance professional, SF Bay Area**

I loved the book. The author's approach is refreshingly relatable. It feels like the examples are from my daily life at home and at work. I feel confident that I can apply the techniques detailed in the book in my everyday work too, not just while preparing for negotiations. For example when I'm creating a proposal or a presentation.

The book cleverly blends theory with simple examples, so it is easily understood. The structure of the text also makes for very easy

Revised Edition

Negotiation Quotient

Opening the Door to a Successful Deal

ANUJ JAGANNATHAN

NEGOTIATION QUOTIENT

Original edition published in 2019 by Beyond Publishing
Revised Edition 2022 by Propelurs Publishing, Propelurs Consulting Private Limited
Copyright @2022 by Anuj Jagannathan

All rights reserved.
Published by Propelurs Consulting Private Limited, No. 4 Retreat Apartments, Raja Rangaswamy Ave, Thiruvanmiyur, Chennai 600041, India
Ph: +91 6380060041
Website: www.propelurs.com/bookpublishing
Printed by Goteti Graphics, Chennai, India or by Amazon Print on Demand service

ISBN: Paperback: 978-1-7356137-0-3

No part of this book may be reproduced, distributed, or transmitted in any form or by any means, including photocopying, recording, or other electronic or mechanical methods, without the prior written permission of the author/publisher, except in the case of brief quotations embodied in book reviews and certain other noncommercial uses permitted by copyright law. For permission requests, write to the publisher addressed "Attention: Permissions for use," at info@propelurs.net.

This book has been published with all the efforts taken to make the material error-free after the consent of the author. However, the author and the publisher do not assume and hereby disclaim any liability to any party for any loss, damage, or disruption caused by errors or omissions, where such errors or omissions result from negligence, accident or any other cause.

Due to the dynamic nature of the internet, some web addresses or links in the ebook may have changed since publication. Reach out to the author for any questions.

reading. So, we are not lost in the flow like it happens with some of the books. The illustrations work almost like a cheat sheet for quick reference. I have found this very useful, because when trying to apply new techniques, it is great to have quick references.

It is a great book to have in your collection. I'd definitely recommend it to my friends and colleagues.
                                      -A senior product manager, Phoenix

It is a fantastic resource for anyone. University students getting ready for professional careers to understand concepts and process of Negotiation, young executives in early career stage looking for utilising the conceptual and practical tools hone their negotiation skills and mid-career executives wanting to advance their negotiation skills by making use of the process, techniques and case studies explained by the author.

It is pertinent to recall here that a large section of businessmen goes for entering into contract with third parties, on varied subjects, without sufficient preparation or even an exposure to the nuances of negotiation in the modern business world. To all of them, this book would definitely be a hands-on trainer to guide to conclude a successful and sustaining negotiation.
              -A retired professor and college principal, India

Anuj is a highly knowledgeable and skilled negotiations trainer. I had the luxury of attending a few of his workshops. His creative ways and skills builder tactics helped me learn how to refine my style to negotiate successfully and ethically in any situation. In his book Negotiation Quotient, Anuj did an excellent job of illustrating his influencing techniques and approach to negotiations process by offering strategies and real life examples! As an added bonus at the end of the book Anuj included a skills assessment and checklist for negotiation process which I found very useful! I highly recommend this book to anyone, regardless of skill level, who is looking to enhance their negotiation skills!
                         -A procurement professional, SF Bay Area

Il y a IQ , EQ et NQ

I just finished the Negotiation Quotient by Anuj Jagannathan and highly recommend it for those looking to expand their knowledge of Negotiation and Influence techniques. The book is full of professional and personal examples that illustrate key techniques and concepts.

-A Senior Tax Advisor, Morocco (LinkedIn)

FOREWORD

And then everything was shut down—no travel, no office, no classroom. Not even a walk in the park. Like many of us, I will remember 2020 as the year of renegotiating my life. The global pandemic forced me to rethink what I had been doing the past six years. I am a professor at the National University of Singapore, and my job is to bring people together for meaningful learning experiences. It's not exactly what you do when a highly infectious and lethal virus is spreading across borders, cities, and neighborhoods at disconcerting speed.

It was around this time that I took to heart one of the key tenets of negotiation: different situations warrant different behaviors and approaches. Throughout my years of studying and working in the field of conflict resolution, I learned that there is no unique way to negotiate successfully. Certainly, some tools and techniques can have universal application, but cultures, behaviors, beliefs, histories, and experiences shape human reaction in negotiation. Awareness, adaptation, and empathy are the main assets of skillful negotiators.

Fast forward several months. I learned how to adapt to the new context and was now ready to launch my first digital course in negotiation for the global learning platform Emeritus. It turned out to be a thrilling experience that brought me in touch with hundreds of passionate professionals and learners whose interest in negotiation skills reinvigorated my passion for teaching. In my journey I was lucky enough to meet Anuj Jagannathan, who played the essential role of co-curating and facilitating my digital course. It didn't take long for us to realize we were sharing the same ideas of what makes an effective negotiator.

What are those ideas? You will have to read Anuj's book to find out. But allow me to share three reasons why I think this book is a valuable resource for anyone who aims to develop negotiation skills. First of all, while working with Anuj I quickly realized we both shared a healthy skepticism for negotiation handbooks that promise you to learn "how to always get what you want" or "the five steps to successful negotiation that will change your life." *Negotiation Quotient* does not make such promises. It is a book that honestly and humbly tells you that knowledge and expertise come with patience and practice. The more you apply negotiation skills, the better you become. The more situations you face, the better you'll be able to address different challenges.

The second fundamental reason I enjoyed this book is its emphasis on process. Preparation, engagement, and closure comprise the essential elements, and breaking down the process in phases will help you balance your negotiation act. Clearly, the ways you prepare, engage, and close will make the difference between a happy or unhappy outcome. The book guides you through the process of negotiation, offering a plethora of daily-life examples which will help you to empathize with and learn from different experiences. What's more, the book recounts cases in which negotiation did not go as planned. Learning from failures is as important as learning from successes. In fact, failures are precious opportunities to learn and improve ourselves.

Finally, Anuj and I share the view that negotiation is both a science and an art. Certainly, negotiation is not like math – two plus two is not always four. A wealth of studies have shown us what works and does not work in certain circumstances, providing us with useful tools and techniques which are deftly explained here in this book. At the same time, negotiation is about mindset. The mindset of an effective negotiator is adaptable, open to learning, empathic, and culturally sensitive. A good negotiator is predisposed to understand that behaviors and beliefs are essential in human experience and thus inclined to consider points of view, perspectives, and perceptions. With such a mindset in place, the negotiator is able to adapt the tools and techniques to achieve the objectives. Here's where you can appreciate the importance of preparation. Negotiation is hard work. It requires studying the issue, collecting information, and learning about your counterpart. Preparation does not solve your negotiation problems, but it does make you prepared and poised to navigate through uncertainties. In brief, such a mindset enhances your power.

Practice, Process, and Preparation: These 3 P's for skillful negotiation are well described in Anuj's book, encouraging you to balance the science and the art of negotiation. It gives you the necessary food-for-thought to go out there and engage in meaningful negotiation experiences. And the more you negotiate, the greater your negotiation quotient will be.

Prof. Francesco Mancini
Vice Dean Exec Education
and Associate Professor in Practice,
Lee Kuan Yew School of Public Policy,
National University of Singapore

• • •

Over the course of my career I've engaged in hundreds, perhaps even thousands, of business-related negotiations–and it wasn't until I finished this book that I realized how unbalanced many of the key players are in their approaches. Anuj is genius in his breakdown of successful negotiations into three phrases: as this offers a very practical place for readers to start when self-assessing for areas of improvement.

In the world of business and negotiation, it can be difficult to remember that every negotiator has a performance gap – an opportunity to improve. There is no shame in that; it's part of the experience. Negotiation Quotient not only helps readers embrace this fact but does an exceptional job at teaching negotiators how to improve. His case studies highlight successes and failures – a rare, but invaluable, find in books about negotiation.

It's this powerful dichotomy - the dynamic lessons learned from success and failure – combined with practical tools for assessing self-improvement that make Negotiation Quotient a must read for all negotiators seeking measurable progress in their performance.

Kwame Christian Esq., M.A.
Managing Director,
The American Negotiation Institute
Ohio, U.S.A.

PREFACE

In the <u>first edition</u> of *Negotiation Quotient*, we reviewed what it takes to enhance our ability to negotiate using the concept of "Balance of Negotiation," indicating balance of the science of negotiation (represented by the key phases - *prepare, engage and close*) with the art of negotiation (appropriate behaviors and effective use of influencing/persuading techniques) to achieve a desirable end result.

I often get asked why negotiation is important. The answer is that we frequently engage in the process of negotiating to achieve desired outcomes, possibly multiple times a day. As negotiation is omnipresent, it is a critical skill for everybody to enhance. In fact, the earlier we are aware and start to develop our negotiating abilities, the greater the benefits we can get from successful negotiation. Mastering the skill requires considerable effort and can be achieved by developing or enhancing your negotiation quotient.

While the inspiration for the first edition of this book came from a deep interest in the topic of negotiation, the need for this revised edition arose from several important lessons acquired since the first edition. I am thankful to all the readers who enjoyed reading the original edition, reviewed the book and shared feedback that could add value to the book. Feedback is gold. Since this feedback directly helps to make the book better, it is important to pass on the benefits to readers.

I endeavor to generate constant value and want to take the opportunity to provide the readers with additional value via this revised edition. Herein I build on negotiation theories and concepts with relevant anecdotes and examples, many of these from my personal daily life-experiences as well as those narrated by colleagues, friends and family members. We all read about successful deals and negotiations that happen at a diplomatic and organizational level, but I have showcased examples that happen in daily life. Furthermore, while it is important to learn from successful negotiation stories that generate a positive feeling and provide insights into some smart strategies, it is equally vital to learn from situations where the negotiation did not go as anticipated. I have incorporated many such cases, which provide a useful perspective for dealing with negotiations that don't meet expectations. Readers will be able to closely align with the experiences highlighted in this edition to enhance their negotiation abilities.

In this edition, there are some stories that relate to negotiations involving kids and young adults. The psychology of influencing works differently with kids and young adults and striking the right chord with them becomes critical. As parents, we often try several different ways with varying degrees of success. It is useful to understand the psychology that makes the difference for the kids and young adults and enables accomplishment of the objective.

Since publishing the first edition of Negotiation Quotient, I have published a book for kids and young adults to make them better negotiators. <u>We Can Negotiate Too!</u> is a book to make kids aware of the importance of negotiation as early as possible. As they start to grow older, they should learn and enhance their negotiation quotient. The sooner they acquire and enhance this critical skill, the larger the value they will generate in their lives. As parents and educators, we need to focus on providing the children an opportunity to become powerful negotiators.

Different situations warrant the application of pertinent behaviors and techniques, and this is where a deep understanding of these behaviors and techniques, along with regular practice, will create effective negotiations. Every opportunity to negotiate is a valuable learning experience for the future. Even if the full negotiation process does not apply to each situation, it is beneficial to practice and hone the skills that are applicable in the specific case.

At the end of this book, I have revised the chapter "My Negotiation Journey" to further illustrate how my complete lack of awareness of structured negotiation turned into a deep exploration and interest in the topic. I have had the opportunity over the last couple of years to share my perspectives and help multiple people in generating awareness and enhancing the skill.

On multiple occasions, friends and contacts ask the question "Why negotiation?" when I discuss my efforts in this topic. I strongly believe that negotiation is a skill that is highly relevant across the board, but it is not adequately taught to everybody. When I introduce the structure to the negotiation process and skills needed to be successful to the participants of my workshop, they are amazed that they should have learned this long ago. I hope all readers will gain meaningful insights and will be able to effectively utilize the learning from the theories, techniques, and examples presented in this book.

INDEX

FOREWORD 7
PREFACE 11
INTRODUCTION 17
CHAPTER 1 Salient Insights of Negotiation 21
CHAPTER 2 The Balance of Negotiation 27
CHAPTER 3 Prepare 32
CHAPTER 4 Engage 77
CHAPTER 5 Close 92
CHAPTER 6 Behaviors 97
CHAPTER 7 Strategic Influencing Techniques 131
CHAPTER 8 My Negotiation Journey 160
REFERENCES 164
ACKNOWLEDGEMENTS 167
APPENDIX A Influencing Skills Assessment 169
APPENDIX B Checklist for Negotiation Process* 176

INTRODUCTION

For a few months since the launch of the first edition of *Negotiation Quotient*, I have been reflecting on negotiation scenarios that commonly occur during the course of a day. On several days, I have kept a log of my daily negotiations. Negotiations occur every day around us. On a regular day, we negotiate a few times a day. In my case, my calculations showed that I am in negotiations on an average about four times a day. The number of negotiations increases if we have an out-of-normal day. Uncertainties, contingencies and additional decisions lead to more negotiations. Do you know how many times you negotiate in a day?

The bigger question is: Are you aware that you are negotiating? Most times, we do not realize we are negotiating. We think it is just a conversation on standard day-to-day topics that we all deal with. Absolutely! That is the point. We all deal with negotiations multiple times in a day but might not associate a negotiation approach to these conversations. In any conversation where each party looks for a particular outcome, it becomes a negotiation. It might be a five-minute conversation, or it could last a few hours or even days.

Let me share an example where a negotiation lasted a few weeks. It was a Sunday morning in early January a few years ago. The important topic of discussion between me and my wife at the breakfast table revolved around the big question: "Where do we go for our tenth anniversary vacation in the summer?" Planning a vacation is never easy, and it becomes even more critical when it is a big occasion.

"How about a cruise to Alaska or a visit to Europe?" my wife suggested. These were among the top choices on our growing list of holiday options. One exotic holiday that was on my mind was an African safari in Serengeti, Tanzania. "Let's go to Serengeti," I responded. "And remember, it has been on the list for ten years now." Flashback to ten years ago: I had proposed an African safari for our honeymoon trip, but not being a common honeymoon destination, it didn't win the vote.

"Are you sure? The kids are still too young," my wife replied. I immediately recognized that this was going to be a crucial point of contention in the negotiation for the African safari. It goes without saying that I had to get a stamp of approval from my family to make it happen.

My wife's concerns primarily arose from her fears regarding safety and health in the remote African safari, compounded by the fact that we were traveling a long distance away from home. Her risk preference was low due to the concern regarding the welfare of little children traveling with us. I responded, "I understand your concerns, and safety and health considerations are also very important for me." It was paramount to understand all her requirements and build a package to meet her interests and address her questions.

Over the next few days, we carefully assessed all aspects of the trip. We planned the trip in a way that my wife and kids would come to Africa from India, as they had already planned a trip to meet family in India. This way, the travel would be shorter and would address the concerns of the long-distance travel from California to Africa. On African safari trips, it is good to have more company. After a discussion with my parents, I suggested that they join us on the trip so that we could have their company and support. As preparation is key in any negotiation, I pulled all available information from the detailed research and analysis I undertook on the internet. I realized that providing my wife with the detailed information about a safari trip would make her feel more comfortable. I showed her the stimulating videos to highlight the attractiveness of the location. Additionally, we read comments and blogs from travelers to Africa for guidance for the trip. Several articles were available that specifically addressed safety aspects on safari trips. This meticulous preparation helped ease some of the initial concerns.

After analyzing several travel package options, I booked a package with adequate assurances of safety with a travel company referred through family connections. We opted for the best lodges and hotels to avoid security issues. The trip would not only include a safari trip, but also a visit to the city of Dar-es-Salaam and the island of Zanzibar. I realized that in order to reach an agreement, certain concessions had to be made, such as booking higher priced hotels and resorts.

Having made all the necessary arrangements and creating solutions that were mutually acceptable, it was possible to create a positive frame of reference to make the negotiation easier. Over a period of six weeks of discussions, we concluded the negotiation that helped build solutions for all parties. In March I went ahead and made the payment for the trip. We were all set for our once-in-a-lifetime family safari trip.

This is one example of a negotiation that we all face on a regular basis. Typically, a host of such examples come our way every day, and it is important how we deal with the situations in the most effective manner. The objective is to achieve the desired results, keeping in mind the interests of all parties involved in the negotiation. Negotiation is not always about the best deal or a winning proposal. Negotiation is about the best outcome that accomplishes objectives and provides a feeling of satisfaction to both or all parties.

So, how is this book different? While there are several books on negotiation, this one provides daily life cases and examples that provide perspectives that the readers can relate with and offer unique learning opportunities. On several occasions, I have asked my friends and colleagues to share their negotiation experiences. This book outlines many of these anecdotes and examples that will resonate with readers.

In my workshops, some of the participants have expressed that they might not be able to use the skills immediately. My view is that these skills can be applied right away. These are useful in all aspects of life. A good understanding of the skills and techniques and consistent practice will help polish the negotiation quotient. As with any other skill, building the tools and learning the tricks is only the first step towards achieving the goal to excel in the skills. Constantly keeping the skills at the back of the mind and analyzing when and how they are used or can be used will lead to successful application. Another concern raised by some people is that negotiation is difficult, and you never know how the other party will react. As with anything else you do, the best results come when you put in all the effort and enjoy the process. I advise them that the *feel-good factor* is vital to the negotiation process.

Many instances call for quick decision-making and compromises, but at the same time it is critical to apply the proper process of negotiation and use the most effective behaviors and techniques for maximum benefit. In the chapters that follow, I highlight the key concepts as a part of the negotiation process and present the appropriate behaviors and a wide array of techniques that can be applied to achieve the objectives.

CHAPTER 1
Salient Insights of Negotiation

The negotiation process can be intriguing. In this chapter, I will highlight seven salient insights of negotiation that will bring to light the basic facets of negotiation. In most instances, these salient insights are misunderstood and become myths or biases of negotiation. My goal is to clarify the position as it relates to these salient facets of negotiation, and by doing so, help people to appreciate that negotiation is a fine blend of science and art.

#1 Negotiation skills are malleable.

Do you face anxiety, nervousness, apprehension or fear when you think of or approach a negotiation? One of the primary reasons for these feelings is that we might not have learned proper negotiation skills. I have good news for everybody reading this book: Negotiation skills are extremely malleable.

So, can anybody learn and apply negotiation skills? Who can attest to this better than myself? Until a few years ago, I never paid much attention to negotiation. By my own negotiation training standards, I was probably one of the worst negotiators and left a lot of value on the table. I have been called out on the lack of adequate negotiation by my wife. I think it might have been because of my inherent *accommodating style* (discussed in detail in Chapter 6 on behaviors). This experience was likely in the back of my mind when I generated interest in this topic. Negotiation as a topic further became a passion after I was exposed to books and exercises as part of my MBA program (details in Chapter 8, "My Negotiation Journey"). Understanding concepts, techniques, and behaviors has helped develop the necessary skills towards becoming a better negotiator. Everyone can become a good negotiator. It only needs investment of some time to learn and apply consistently. It is my mission to teach kids and young adults and help them become better negotiators so that they can benefit from the skills over their long careers and lives.

#2 Creativity is the key to effective solutions.

Most of us approach a negotiation as a conversation that we engage in with the other party, exchanging our requirements and bargaining for an outcome that works for each party. For a long time, this was my approach too. Creativity was not at the top of mind. However, as we saw in salient insight #1 above, learning the skills in negotiating brings creativity in deriving solutions. Skilled negotiators bring out the value for all parties using mutually beneficial solutions.

Let's look at an example. Supplier X received a frantic call from his Customer Y, who stated that they required the parts inventory to reach them by Day 15. This was critical for the customer as they needed to tag the parts and package them on Day 16 for two-day shipping to the end user by Day 18. The supplier needed time until Day 14 to manufacture the parts and a shipping time of two days. So the earliest they could send the parts to the customer was Day 16 with an additional three days to reach the end user - hence resulting in a delay of a day.

The supplier came up with a creative solution, asking the customer if they could tag the parts and package them at their end. Thus, they could send it from their factory on Day 15 to reach the end user on Day 17, a saving of a day. Certainly such a creative solution could result in a win-win-win situation.

#3 Negotiation is not war.

While many of us are aware that negotiation is not war, we often go into the discussion to get the most for ourselves or gain an upper hand. One participant in my workshops said that negotiation for her meant to "prove her point." I did a Google translation for the word "negotiation" into Hindi, and one of the answers provided was "to win." Such feelings and thoughts that come to mind when entering a negotiation can prove detrimental to the effectiveness of your approach and the success of your negotiation.

Negotiation is not a war. Negotiation is not a platform for conflict and gaining an upper hand at the expense of the other. It is an opportunity for the parties to come together and strive to get the best possible results for all as well as an opportunity to resolve conflicts in the best possible manner. In fact, the idea to walk into a negotiation must be that of a collaboration where everybody walks away feeling that they got a deal. Everybody grows together in a collaborative negotiation. If this does not happen, the experience will yield negative feelings.

#4 Price is almost never the primary or only criterion.

Ever wondered how important is the "price" component in a negotiation? "Price" here refers to the price, amount, salary, or any other quantitative aspect in the negotiation. I am surprised that in many conversations or during my workshops, people place a significant emphasis on "price." One of my friends was discussing his preparation for salary negotiation with me. Most of his questions related to maximizing the "number." I asked what the reasons were for his interest in the job. Some reasons were clearly beyond the salary. For example, his interest was in the foray the company was making into an exciting area of technology. In a few cases, if a negotiation is based solely on the price, it is most likely a *distributive approach* to negotiation (a topic we will discuss further in Chapter 3). This approach focuses on dividing the pie, which assumes that there is a pie that needs to be split between the parties. If one party gets 50 percent the other gets 50; if one party gets 60 percent, the other gets 40.

Effective negotiation is about creating solutions that go beyond a distributive approach. Several interests that the parties have can be fulfilled by keeping aside the element of "price." In a recent conversation with a friend, he highlighted how in most conversations he would feel disgruntled because the other party would primarily push further on the price component. Generating value in a deal and thereby creating solutions that deliver the value improve relationships and provide the contentment.

#5 "Walk-away" is also a solution.

It is paramount to point out that not all situations result in a successful negotiation. Not all negotiations go as anticipated. Furthermore, as per the circumstances, not all negotiations need to end up in a deal. Sometimes buyer remorse is worse than reaching a deal. Thus, coming to a compromise is not obligatory. Don't overcommit to a negotiation and be compelled to make a decision.

Negotiations could result in a "walk-away" if parties are not able to reach the desired outcomes. A skilled negotiator is also able to look at the big picture and decide when is a good time to negotiate and to what extent. Having a strong assessment of alternatives will provide the confidence and courage to walk away if circumstances require. Sometimes, in the grand scheme of things, it might not be useful or necessary to negotiate. The smart negotiators know this and deal with every situation differently. Multiple negotiations end up in a walk away.

The "walk-away" can be of two types:
- Interim walk-away, where parties agree to take a break and regroup after a while. They may go back to the drawing board to work further; and
- Final walk-away, where no conclusion or decision can be reached by the parties and the only option is to close off the deal.

#6 Negotiation is being human.

Do you know that there is another big benefit of learning negotiation in addition to helping you make your deals successful? It makes you a better human being. One facet that is often overlooked in a negotiation is the human element. Negotiation is much more than just a conversation with a human being. It is about being human.

In this age of AI and automation, the primary skills that will help one succeed will revolve around being human. This primarily suggests that we need to focus on the other person as much as the matter at hand. We need to have better understanding and empathy, develop trust, and communicate ardently. In a negotiation, it is therefore crucial to develop people skills. One question that might be asked is, "What if we demonstrate the human aspect but the other party does not?" While this is certainly a possibility, it is important to do your best, and by doing so, it will rub off on the other party. What's more, this will also enable us to nurture stronger relationships.

#7 Negotiation is not black or white.

The basic premise of a negotiation is that you can't have a template or checklist to work with for different situations. There might be a list of points to consider but not a specific step-by-step process to follow. Each negotiation is an interplay of strategies and behaviors that are based on the specific case. I was recently grading some negotiation assignments, and my wife asked, "Do you have a standard answer that you can use to quickly grade the assignments?" Of course, the answer is "No." There are no standard answers for negotiation practices and behaviors.

A friend recently mentioned a case where his suggestions at work were dismissed by his higher-level management. I asked what options he had explored in his "negotiation" with management. He mentioned a few options. I suggested a few more options to him. The point is that there are many options since negotiation is not simply black or white. In some cases, biding time is another option. I further suggested that he has to be ready to "strike at the right time." All options have to be explored and implemented.

The dynamics of the circumstances, the people on both sides and their styles, the alternatives, the power and the relationships all govern the effectiveness of the negotiation. In coaching friends and connections on their specific negotiation cases, I lay out the different scenarios that could fall into play.

Ultimately, a blend of the factors presented above will determine the result. If you approach a negotiation advisor for help, don't expect a checklist with steps to take. It's anything but a black or white answer. Good negotiators explore several options and solutions; and determine what could work. They might even try a few strategies simultaneously to determine which of those work as per the situation and circumstances.

CHAPTER 2
The Balance of Negotiation

The negotiation process can be quite intriguing. This chapter gives an overview of the negotiation process that I refer to as the *Balance of Negotiation*. The ability to negotiate with a strong impact depends on the ability to effectively navigate the various stages and multiple steps in the negotiation process. Managing the tacit use of techniques and appropriate demonstration of behavior is paramount.

First, let us understand what negotiation is. In my workshops, when I ask the participants what they understand by negotiation, I frequently hear answers such as - "win-win," "coming to a compromise," and "building trust." However, I occasionally hear "proving your point" or "making sure I win." Are these answers correct? Such answers might be correct, depending on the situation and the type of negotiation. Negotiations occur when the parties have differing objectives and desired outcomes. So, in general, you should strive to achieve the desired outcome from the negotiation exercise, not only for yourself but also for the other party. This is how I describe a negotiation:

Negotiation is an interactive exchange between two or more parties to achieve desired outcomes, individually as well as on an integrative basis.

Now, let's break this down and analyze this description of a negotiation in a bit more detail:

- Negotiation is an interactive exchange between two or more parties. This exchange is important to establish the connection in a negotiation. The interactive exchange could be face-to-face or remote. In Chapter 3 we will look at a different kind of interactive exchange that is prevalent in the current age and which I refer to as "Click-thru" negotiation.
- Achieving desired outcomes is the goal of every negotiation exercise. Outcomes need to be achieved not only for each party individually but also cater to the mutual interests of all parties. As can be expected, the process of achieving the desired outcomes is of key importance. Do we achieve the desired outcome without attention to developing relationships, or do we achieve the outcome while keeping in mind the long-term relationship and mutual interests? The answer is the latter.

Let's note additional key aspects of negotiations below:

- Negotiation is ubiquitous. We are all negotiators already. At times we negotiate multiple times and under different circumstances in a single day. Several times we probably don't even realize we are negotiating. It is therefore important to increase awareness by learning the vital aspects of negotiation. As narrated in some stories over the next few chapters, negotiating starts very early in life. Babies and little kids negotiate. Their approach to negotiating might be limited to yelling, crying, or wailing in different circumstances, based on the situation. As they grow, they add more horsepower to their negotiating abilities by developing better skills through experience. Around the age of eight, kids begin to develop the ability to reason. It is important to keep improving negotiating abilities by developing better skills through learning and experience.

- Negotiation requires an open mind. Not all negotiations go as you expect. Bear in mind that in some situations your negotiation might fail, and either party could walk away if they are not able to achieve their desired outcome. You should not feel bad about a failure in negotiation. Instead, be able to decide when it is a good time to stop. However, a good understanding of the skills, techniques, and consistent practice will help polish your negotiation skills to an extent that you will be able to get a deal that will be closer to your interests. Furthermore, you learn every time you negotiate. The more you practice, the better you will get at negotiating. the adage "Practice makes you perfect"! As with anything else you do, the best results come when you put in the effort and enjoy the process.
- Our negotiating ability is a factor of our individual styles. Enhancing our negotiation skills is a continuous learning process. While we all start with inherent styles, experiences help us mold our style over time. Our style adapts to different situations and circumstances, and our negotiation skills gradually improve. We will discuss in more detail about styles in the chapter on behaviors.

The Balance of Negotiation

Let's visualize a balance scale. On one side of the scale, we have the Science of Negotiation, comprising three distinct phases of the negotiation process: Prepare, Engage, and Close. On the other side of the scale, we have the Art of Negotiation comprising of the necessary behaviors and influencing techniques. In the next few chapters, we will look at each phase of the process in detail, but for now a summary is stated below. All three phases play an equally critical role in the negotiation.

The **Prepare phase** is where important information is gathered and a proper plan is formulated to engage in the negotiation. Just like other aspects of life where proper planning and assembling of available facts plays a key role in the success of our endeavors, success is heavily dependent on the preparation that goes into the start of the negotiation. Even skilled negotiators need to put in adequate time and effort in preparation, as every case is different and has to be dealt with accordingly.

The **Engage phase** determines the most effective way of engaging the other party, depending on the circumstances, and occurs as the next major phase in a negotiation. The amount of effort at the Prepare phase of the negotiation has to be backed up with a proper delivery of the information to the other party or parties in the negotiation. As most will agree, solid preparation can complement but not substitute for the actual engagement in a negotiation.

The **Close phase** occurs when the deal is sealed, thereby reaping the benefit of the results of effective preparation and engagement. No negotiation is final unless it is properly closed. The Close phase also includes any final communications and approvals that might be required to complete the negotiation.

These three phases of negotiation are supported by behaviors and techniques during the entire negotiation process. It is vital to strike the right balance between the phases of negotiation and the appropriate use of behaviors and techniques. The *Balance of Negotiation* demonstrates that a negotiation is an equal blend of science and art. A sound implementation of the process and careful maneuvering of behaviors and techniques results in developing a strong **Negotiation Quotient**.

In the next few chapters, we will dive deeper into the three phases, behaviors, and techniques that are key to the whole negotiation process.

CHAPTER 3
Prepare

"Failing to prepare is preparing for failure."
- **Benjamin Franklin**

The first step in the Balance of Negotiation is the "Prepare" phase. This chapter delves deeper into all aspects of this critical phase where one would lay out the strategy for the negotiation.

I recently conducted a survey inviting thousands of participants to rate themselves on a scale of 1 to 10 to answer one question: Do you prepare adequately before you enter into a negotiation? The results were alarming. Sixty-six percent of around five hundred participants rated themselves 5 or lower in preparation for a negotiation. Now this is not surprising. It just shows that negotiation skills are not commonly taught

How does preparation help? Preparation is key to your negotiating success. It is not meant to make you perfect before you go out and negotiate. However, it helps you create better options, navigate uncertainties and address your deficiencies better. It supports you to deal with conflicts effectively.

The preparation toward an effective negotiation has four primary elements: Approaches to Negotiation; CAV Framework; Assess

Interests (including anchors); and Assess Alternatives. In addition, it is vital to understand the type of negotiation you are involved with and customize the strategies accordingly. Let's first introduce the approaches to negotiation.

Approaches to Negotiation

There are two distinct approaches to negotiations: 1) Distributive and 2) Integrative. Depending on the type of negotiation, the approach will apply, and it is important to understand the differences to be able to identify the appropriate approach applicable and accordingly determine the strategies. The strategies will vary based on the approach that is followed, and it is vital to ensure the assess the approach properly. The incorrect assessment of approach and strategy applied will make the negotiation ineffective.

1) Distributive negotiation

This approach typically involves two parties where the objective is to bargain for a one-time or short-term deal. There is no interest in building a relationship for the longer term. The best way to explain this approach to negotiation is by using the phrase "dividing the pie," which implies that there is a fixed pie, and each party attempts to grab their portion of the pie. If one party gets half, the other gets half. If one gets 60 percent, the other gets 40, and so on.

In this type of negotiation, both parties go hard at each other in terms of the bargaining. So it is highly likely that each party works to get an upper hand in the negotiation at the expense of the other. Ultimately, each party walks away with their share of the pie.

Imagine if one is walking in the crowded market in Shanghai and comes across a new kid's toy. In this situation, the approach to use in the negotiation for the price is likely to be distributive, i.e. the shopkeeper and the customer are both interested in achieving the best price.

Consider another scenario where you are selling your used car. The objective for both the buyer and the seller is to get the best price. There is minimal attempt to understand the interests of the other party or to build solutions that will help the other party.

In many situations where a distributive approach is used in the negotiation, the final outcome is compromise, and parties might walk away not knowing whether they got a good deal.

Several hardball techniques are employed in distributive negotiations. Some of the most common hardball tactics are Good Cop/Bad Cop, Highball or Lowball, Bogey, and Nibble.

- Good Cop/Bad Cop is the use of psychology where two people form a team, one acting as an adversary and one as a friend with the objective to lead the other party in a negotiation or interrogation into believing and agreeing with the "friend."
- Highball (state an extremely high price) or Lowball (state an extremely low price) is to set an anchor so high or low with the primary intent to throw off the other person into believing in the unrealistic anchor.
- Bogey is the tactic to insert a fictitious person or action to influence the other party's behavior.
- Nibble is to put forth some minor interests or ask for small concessions after substantial negotiations are completed but just before closing a deal.

As the name suggests, the Good Cop/Bad Cop tactic is commonly used in police interrogations. However, it is also frequently used in the corporate and professional world. A colleague applied this tactic in a negotiation with a service provider, leading the service provider to believe that they had to add extra resources to the project. The colleague played good cop and another team member played the bad cop. The bad cop started by stating that he believed the service provider might not be able to meet the timelines for a client of their size and volumes. My colleague, however, jumped in to state that they could provide the service provider a chance if they assured that sufficient resources would be employed on the project. The service provider was inclined to believe the "good cop" and committed to additional resources.

To better illustrate the tactic of Highball and Lowball, I would like to share a story that my colleague narrated about a distributive negotiation in Egypt. My colleague was shopping for a local painting with the shopkeeper who at first asked for $1,200 for the painting. My colleague immediately countered with $30. At this stage of the story, it seems unimaginable whether this was a highballing or a lowballing exercise until you hear of the final outcome. When my colleague quoted $30, she did not believe or expect that she would get the painting at that price. But certainly, being in a distributive negotiation, she started off using classic hardball tactics. Another colleague who had joined my colleague in this shopping experience was stunned and whispered that the shopkeeper quoted $1,200 and not $120. Now to the final outcome: after a considerable amount of time spent in the bargaining, the shopkeeper agreed for a price of $60. Clearly a case of highball? It prompts one to think to what heights can people go to in these hardball tactics.

I heard a story recently from a mom where the negotiation between the grandmother and grandson illustrates the hardball tactic known as 'Bogey' very well. The grandmother was trying to influence the child to drink a cup of milk. The grandson was resisting, and his excuse was that the milk was a different brand from the one he likes. The grandmother tried winning the boy over by using all the common techniques used with a child. In the end, a hardball tactic did the trick. The grandmother introduced a bogey by calling the mother and pretending to yell at her, "If you do not bring the kid's preferred milk brand today, you will not be allowed to enter the home." And then she told the child, "Okay, now you can drink this milk for today!" For the child, this was enough to create a positive frame of mind and provide reassurance to drink the milk.

2) Integrative negotiation

This approach to negotiations focuses on developing relationships. The objective is to build solutions that mutually benefit all parties. It is an approach regularly used among friends, family, and business partners where the intent is to sustain long-term partnerships. The best way used to explain this approach to negotiation is by the phrase "growing the pie." In the scenarios where there are multiple issues on the table for negotiation, the integrative approach helps to devise solutions for such multiple points effectively. The notion that the pie is fixed needs to be replaced with growing the pie, the idea that the pie can be expanded such that both parties walk away with a win-win. This is a big change in mindset for most people. This type of negotiation requires bringing out the creativity in thinking.

In an integrative negotiation, parties have to be honest about priorities and open to devising solutions that provide benefits beyond the positions in the negotiation. Constraints also need to be highlighted clearly, so that both parties are fully aware of challenges. In a negotiation where the expectations of one party cannot be met, proper justification for the reasons will ensure that relationships stay intact.

Consider, for example, a negotiation where a CEO of a retail company is considering an investment in a logistics company. The goal of both parties is to develop a partnership that provides mutual benefits, in this case, the growth of the logistics company would help the investment of the retail company.

While the distributive approach works well in certain specific situations, the integrative approach is the most common and effective in negotiations. The focus of this book is primarily on the integrative approach. Acknowledging the approach to negotiation is an essential step in the Prepare phase of a negotiation.

• • •

The Competency-Ability-Value (CAV) Framework

In the Prepare phase, one of the critical actions is to evaluate the merits that one can bring to the table. Being proficient at what you do is equally as important as being able to articulate and demonstrate your proficiency. Concerted effort in compiling the criteria to showcase the merits will yield the anticipated results in a negotiation.

This gives me the opportunity to introduce the framework for the Prepare phase that will lead the way in formulating necessary strategies for your negotiation. This framework is called **The CAV Framework**. As is evident from the name, there are three primary facets of this framework – Competency, Ability, and Value. I have presented this framework and its applicability at workshops with my clients with meaningful results.

Let's now look at these facets supported with examples. These facets can be applied to every integrative negotiation, but might not be as pertinent in a distributive negotiation.

Competency

This facet is to state "what" is on offer, i.e. what are the products, services or an idea that you bring to the table. The CAV Framework could be applied to an idea as well. In every negotiation, the primary goal would be to demonstrate what is being provided to the other party and what are the key features and benefits. This goal is achieved through proper planning and readiness as a part of the Prepare phase. For example, an organization can spotlight their portfolio of tangible products or services. The key is to identify the strong points in the negotiation by listing down all the items on offer and highlighting the impact of your product or service to the other party.

My experience of negotiating with friends and contacts on hosting my workshop in their organization is a basic example to explain the CAV framework. When I am discussing with clients about organizing my negotiation workshop, I spell out the topics I will cover in the workshop and why those are important for the participants. These are key aspects that call out the merits of the content in my workshops. This is the "Competency" facet of the workshop.

Ability

This facet states the "how" of what you offer, i.e., the extraordinary ability in the delivery of the competency. "Ability" is emphasized by outlining the distinguishing features and unique aspects of the products, services or ideas. Any product or service cannot fully justify its competency aspect unless it is uniquely delivered to the other party. So this facet can be inferred as the "intangible" characteristics of your products or services. Special attributes to mention are: security, safety, accuracy, and speed, among others. While these are the direct features of the products or services, often parties in a negotiation also speak highly of their organization's values (such as the brand, strong partnerships, ethics, privacy, diversity, corporate social responsibility, etc.), depending on the industry to which they belong, to demonstrate their special ability. Ability is vital in ensuring that the competencies are provided in the best possible manner. Look at the case of Facebook a few years ago, where the supreme efforts in developing the excellent Competency of its product led to a relaxation of its privacy controls. This proved extremely costly to the company and its reputation.

As an example highlighting Ability, I noted the comments made by a CEO of a large Fortune 500 company who used a special approach to reinforce the company's "Ability". The CEO identified enhancement areas in the way the company is serving the customers and called out specific measures the company is taking to improve on those areas. The CEO mentioned to the customers that the company is devising a plan to strengthen its ability around the key focus areas and improve the experience for the customers.

Continuing on the workshop example, in addition to showcasing what I will cover, I present the unique aspects and the approach of delivery. Specifically, this refers to the captivating features built in the workshop, such as real-life stories from people like the participants, videos to make the content stimulating, and exercises and simulations to encourage interaction. This is the "Ability" facet of the workshop.

Value
This facet refers to "why" the competency and ability matter to the other party, i.e. the value that is derived by them in the negotiation. In a negotiation, while the emphasis is on the product or service offered and the way it is delivered, it is vital to stress the additional value or bonus that the other party can derive. As an example, in a negotiation, value can be created by extending attractive discounts or giving away some products or services.

Finally, to close on the earlier workshop example, complementing the information on what I will cover and how it will be delivered, I present the additional value for the organization (such as providing a session for free, specifically customizing the workshop for the organization, or offering free coaching to participants outside of the classroom) that goes above and beyond the "Competency" and "Ability" facets.

As mentioned earlier, the CAV Framework applies to all situations where you are preparing for negotiations regarding product or services. This framework can similarly be used in negotiations promoting an idea or influencing a concept. An example from one of my workshop participants suggests that the CAV framework can also be applied to ideas.

As this is an interesting framework, it is best to explain this with an example that we all can relate to. Let's take the example of how Google would apply CAV Framework for its search business:

Competency - To be able to provide search results for any question that a user asks or any information that a user seeks from the information available across the millions of pages on the web at less than the time for a blink of the eyes. A strong competency indeed which provides what customers need and highlights the benefits of the service.

Ability - In addition to an impactful Competency, the Ability helps Google further. This includes: Pagerank algorithm that produces best results based on the best information, Suggesting search phrases based on machine learning, talkback functionality etc.

Value - Finally, even though Google might have great Competency and Ability, is there any additional Value it can provide to the users? Absolutely! It provides the best results curated for users. For example, you do not need to search multiple times for information related to an event such as Tokyo Olympics or cricket world cup. When you search for the name of the event, it provides all relevant information in one place such as games, medals, scores etc. Also, there is the Google Alerts feature that a user can sign up for and receive search results on their email even without going to search. All this is additional value that users can get. All in all, the CAV Framework makes it irresistible for the user to use Google.

One of my workshop participants shared her experience of using skills learned in the workshop to a real-life case. Her example typifies the use of CAV Framework for an idea. In the organization, there is a long list of robotic automation projects that are prioritized based on the impact to the organization. In order to get a project to the top of the list, the real impact must be demonstrated, so the participant started preparing the case for her negotiation to support why her project should take precedence over other projects.

The "Competency" facet of this project was to present the case for automation of a financial reporting process. The idea of automating the critical global, monthly consolidated reporting process emphasizes the importance of the idea.

The "Ability" facet of this automation idea is to outline how this automation will work to achieve the desired outcome of automating the financial reporting process. The participant invested her time to record her process steps using a recorder software showing how every step can be automated. Her efforts to show detailed steps in the automation would make the robotic automation implementation easier. The "Ability" facet also comes from the participant's extra efforts to facilitate the implementation of the idea. In this case, the participant used the Vested technique (which we will review in Chapter 7) by aligning on this idea with the managers in her team and the broader teams. This enabled her to garner the support for her idea when all the projects are lined up for prioritization.

And finally, the "Value" framework of the automation idea was well prepared and articulated. The participant identified that in a monthly reporting process of five days, every hour is valuable. This automation will reduce the reporting time by eight hours. Additionally, this reporting has beneficial downstream impact on broader teams that use this reporting. So it results in faster availability of information for the other teams. These benefits helped to provide leverage to the "Competency" and "Ability" aspects of the negotiation.

We can apply the CAV Framework to a new job interview as well. Let's look at how.

Competency - When you are in an interview, it is understood that you would highlight your competency for the role by stating your qualifications, experience and the value you can bring to the company and role.

Ability - In addition to having a good Competency, you can highlight special or unique aspects such as specific experience in leadership roles outside of work, association roles or membership, any additional experience that you bring to the organization etc. These are over and above your core competency.

Value - Good combination of Competency and Ability gives you a strong potential to be hired. However, additional Value will easily take you past the finishing line. Value could be presented by sharing what you can bring that is beyond what the organization expects. For example, if you bring expertise in specific areas and could train employees, experience in mentoring employees, strong industry network, etc.

As you can see from these examples, the CAV Framework is applicable to any product or service you want to highlight or any idea or proposal you want to share. Use this when you prepare for your next proposal.

In the next two sections, we will discuss two vital elements of the Prepare phase: Assess Interests and Assess Alternatives.

• • •

Assess Interests

I often get asked the question, "What is one thing that you would like to mention that people should know about a negotiation?" While there are several aspects in consideration for a successful negotiation, one of the most important contributors is the ability to focus on interests. A primary objective is not only to know our own interests, but also to understand the other party's interests. In most cases of a distributive approach, there are positions on both sides and focusing on interests might not be useful. However, this is paramount in the integrative approach. Assessing interests drives the development of a longer-term trust-based relationship, which is critical in integrative negotiations. Before we dig deeper into this, let's take a simple example to understand Positions and Interests.

A mother and child are negotiating about the child joining a swimming class. As you know, when a child starts to learn swimming, there are apprehensions associated with the unknown. So in this example, let's look at positions and interests.

Positions: The kid's position is that she does not want to go for swimming, and the mother's position is that she wants the kid to go to the class. These become the primary criteria for a negotiation based on positions.

Interests: The mother and kid both have the underlying interests behind their positions. The mother highlights her interests that kids should learn how to swim, as it is a life-saving skill, good exercise, and lots of fun. The mother wants the kid to learn swimming, so that she can enjoy it with family and friends. On the other hand, after discussing further, the kid explains her interests: she is scared of deep water, she does not want to learn with many kids, the water is cold, etc.

Analyzing the above example, both sides have valid interests, but they need to understand the other party's interests, too. In this case, since this is a negotiation between a child and her mother, it would be the mother's prerogative to address all the interests to achieve a win-win.

This simple example clearly provides the distinction between positions and interests. Negotiating over positions is ineffective. It often results in a compromise or a walk-away. The results are not always ideal. Conversely, negotiations with interests in mind often result in positive results and mutual gains.

A classic example of positions and interests that is frequently used in all spheres in the negotiation world is the story of two sisters and an orange.

There are several versions of the story, but the essence of the story emphasizes the concept of interests in a negotiation. Two sisters were both arguing over who would get the last remaining orange. In this case, a compromise was reached by the mother to split the orange in half, so they both get a fair share. So was this a "win-win" situation? Apparently, the answer is no. The essence of this story is beyond the compromise. The story is about assessing the interests of the sisters. If there was an attempt to find out what each sister wanted to do with the orange prior to the compromise – one sister wanted to eat the fruit and the other wanted the rind to bake a cake – the focus could have been on the interests of each party, resulting in a "win-win", since both would have achieved their objective.

A colleague was complaining that she regularly has to negotiate with her kids and it is challenging, as they always keep asking for different things. At this point, I mentioned that if she was having similar discussions with adults, she would be doing everything to come to a solution that worked for all parties, so why would she not do that with her kids? After all, it is also a negotiation, and the same principles should apply. She should understand the interests of the kids and build solutions that mutually cater to her kids and herself.

As a negotiation is most effective when the interests of both parties are brought to the table to discuss and a concerted effort is made to cater to these interests, it is important to prepare for the negotiation with a focus on assessing one's own and the other party's interests. This is significant in the case of integrative negotiations, but could be applied in distributive negotiations, too. Some of the following would help in this process:

- Believe that a win-win is possible, and stretch your imagination to derive mutually beneficial solutions.
- List your interests and their interests. Often, a list of multiple interests can be derived from detailed analysis and understanding of objectives.
- Make an attempt to understand or gauge the other party's interests based on all available information and discussions.
- Some of the other party's interests might be implicit, so it is crucial to explore and build solutions for the implicit interests. As is evident from integrative approach to negotiations, it is also possible to build some solutions that the other party might not be aware of. This results in "growing the pie".
- Determine the key decision-maker on their side to cater to his/her interests.
- Prepare creative solutions based on your and other party's interests. Devise multiple solutions that you could offer as a package to address their interests.

- Assess if any points could create conflict and disagreement, and prepare solutions to handle those.

A participant in a workshop asked, "How do you estimate value in a negotiation deal?"

Value depends on what your interests are in the negotiation. So in a nutshell, the meaning of value created depends on what is accomplished in the negotiation. In some cases it could mean a higher monetary benefit but in others it might not. The monetary aspect might be minor as against the other interests. For example, let's look at a story from April this year. A friend was interviewing with Nvidia, a strong company. His current company and role were not attractive and sustainable. His new role would be in areas that would bring long term benefits. Furthermore, he would get better work-life advantages as Nvidia was very close to his home. So overall, these interests meant that monetary aspects were not the primary value generating drivers.

In a negotiation, value is created by generating solutions that will help the other party. So assess their interests in your discussions with them and if you would be able to provide what is important to the other party. This will bring them significant value.

Now, to support the topic of interests a bit further, let's look at some stories and examples.

Renouncing a lucrative revenue stream for long-term partnership

I have developed this example from various articles available online. In 2010, Microsoft sued Motorola for patent infringement over Android devices. Based on this, Microsoft built a legal authority and started collecting license revenue from Motorola and other Android OEM manufacturers. This was a billion-dollar revenue stream for Microsoft.

In September 2015, Microsoft and Google (Google had since acquired Motorola in 2013) agreed to dismiss about 20 pending patent infringement suits between them. This provided the exemption from patent infringement to Google and other OEMs. Additionally, both companies agreed to partner in patent and other areas. Microsoft was willing to forego the lucrative revenue stream from patent licensing.

So what prompted Microsoft in taking this extreme stance?

One big development during this time was that Satya Nadella had taken over the reins of the company in September 2014. Under Nadella, Microsoft was looking at integrative solutions as a part of this decision and wanted to partner with OEMs to develop trust for long-term relationships. The opportunity lost from such partnerships could be much higher than the license fees it was collecting. Microsoft saw the opportunity to influence the OEMs to pre-install all apps on Android devices for a lower or fully waived license fee. For an OEM, even $3 to $5 per device could add up to a lot of money every year.

The Android ecosystem grew to a massive scale between 2010 and 2015, and this was the best way for Microsoft to make their platform-agnostic apps reach the customers and offer a seamless experience across any device. This was noted as one of the primary interests for Microsoft in their blog post in February 2016. Microsoft announced that a significant number of Android-based device manufacturers packaged its software and apps out of the box. Nick Parker, corporate vice president of the OEM division, confirmed that Android apps and services were already pre-installed by 74 hardware partners in 25 countries. Microsoft stated in its blog post: "In a mobile-first, cloud-first world, it's mobility of the experiences that matter to people, and devices are critical to bringing this to life for consumers, businesses, developers, and IT. Our aspiration at Microsoft is to continue to build and grow a vibrant community of billions of people who love and rely on Microsoft experiences, on any device, across all aspects of their daily lives."

An intriguing experience results in positive outcome
I wanted to present my view of an intriguing story of Amazon's experience with tax authorities in the U.K., and how focusing on interests was one of the primary aspects in this experience.

This case relates to the U.K. Value Added Tax (VAT). In October 2017, U.K. authorities claimed that VAT fraud among online shopping marketplaces has resulted in losses to Her Majesty's Revenue and Customs (HMRC) of £1 billion or more every year. U.K. lawmakers specifically called out Amazon and eBay for not taking enough measures to prevent the VAT fraud. In the midst of all this, in October 2017, HMRC awarded its cloud services contract to Amazon, resulting in a local cloud services company losing the business of HMRC, which accounted for 85 percent of its revenue. This move by HMRC was widely criticized. Margaret Hodge, a Member of Parliament said, "They say they want to be tough on tax avoidance, but they use our money to give contracts to some of the world's biggest and most immoral tax avoiders." HMRC, on the other hand, said that the decision was made to have better cloud capabilities at a significantly lower cost that would benefit the taxpayers.

Interestingly, a few months later in April 2018, both Amazon and eBay agreed to partner with HMRC to share merchants' data that would help cut down VAT tax evasion. This was a significant outcome in this long-standing debate with HMRC. This was absolutely a case where HMRC and Amazon understood each other's interests and acted to build the best possible solutions to address those interests. Amazon managed to convince U.K. authorities that its superior cloud services helped HMRC and taxpayers, and at the same time agreed to do everything possible to help the authorities with their objective to tackle a long-standing issue of VAT evasion and be regarded as being a good corporate citizen.

Genuinely need resources?
A common case of negotiation in a corporate environment is the request for additional staff in the team. It is generally understood that to successfully increase headcount, one has to go through a difficult negotiation. So what does it take to request additional resources?

Looking at this from the lens of an executive leading a group of departments, it is imperative for certain departments that have critical projects to get additional headcount. For the other departments, while increased volume of work is the most common reason to request more headcount, it is important for department managers to support the request with sound analysis. At the same time, the executive might have received instructions that the overall headcount would need to remain flat for the organization. The managers need to understand the interests of the executive and be able to align with the overall objectives. They need to be aware of critical projects happening across the departments. If a manager's department does not meet the criteria for critical projects, the increase in headcount might be a difficult ask. In fact, some managers would be expected to decrease the headcount in their team to help with the increase in other departments supporting critical projects. This is the way it works in most negotiations involving headcount.

If managers believe that they have a genuine need for additional headcount in their department, they should come prepared to explain how they will operate if they do not get the additional resources. This is the assessment of alternatives (that we will review in the next section). In this assessment, some managers come back with proper analysis of all the activities ranked from high to low priority. They are able to demonstrate that without more resources, some of the low-priority activities cannot be completed or will need to be deferred. Managers need to be able to explain the risks and potential consequences that are associated with eliminating or deferring the low-priority activities for executives to be able to make an informed decision. To make the negotiation easier, the managers also need to analyze what benefits can be gained through automating processes, removing redundant steps, building efficiencies, etc. These benefits can free up resources to take on newly added work.

As mentioned earlier, proper understanding of overall objectives and timelines of critical requirements from the executive will help managers make better decisions. If reducing headcount is certain, a commitment to reduction later in the year, such as in the third or last quarter might meet expectations of the executive and allow enough time for the managers to prepare for the eventuality. In some cases, while some managers might need to give up headcount, they might be able to request temporary staff to help with wrapping up any pending activities. These are valid solutions to build in the negotiation process. Coming armed with solid preparation and strong analysis enables the managers to negotiate effectively.

First-of-its-kind, unique concept for a popular store
This is a story from the small town of Dublin in California, U.S.A. After years of negotiations, the IKEA store in Dublin is expected to become a reality with a city council approval received in November 2018. The planned 317,000-square-foot store on a 27-acre site is expected to be ready in three years.

Along the long and difficult path to the approval, IKEA faced challenges from the city and residents. Concerns were mostly around the store's impact on convenience and appearance, including: traffic, vast parking lots that could appear in front of the store, and the dominant blue and yellow colors. As a result, IKEA made it a priority to address these interests and made major changes to its proposed plans. It scrapped the option to build the large surface parking lot and instead opted for an underground parking lot. Addressing a specific call-out from the residents' community, the company also added designs that include a gray mesh-like feature and glass on its facade. So this IKEA comes with a twist. It would be the only IKEA store in the country to have colors other than the iconic blue and yellow. In addition, IKEA committed to investing $420,000 for a significant artistic feature that Mayor David Haubert said would add a "wow" factor to the site.

So did IKEA really need to make all these changes? No. In 2004, the then-city council approved a commercial plan that included a 317,000-square-foot IKEA store. So if the City Council now decided to reject the project, IKEA had a right to move ahead with a regular planned store. So the alternatives (see next section) for the city were weak or non-existent. IKEA would not have been willing to accommodate all the interests if they were denied the approval. "The plan throughout has been if this were disproved, we're coming back. And we're going to come back with a project that the public probably won't like as much, that this council probably won't like as much. But it's a project that …has essentially been approved before," IKEA's attorney David Blackwell said. The city council's alternative would have been to fight a lawsuit with IKEA, which would have proved too costly for the city. But IKEA preferred to partner with the city and the community to develop a solution that works for all. A city would be happy to have a partner like IKEA.

A significant statement was made by Angele Robinson-Gaylord, president of U.S. Property at IKEA that highlights IKEA's focus for mutual benefit: "It's been a long road, but the work we've done together has created a stronger blueprint for a retail property that serves the needs of the community and represents the kind of development of which we can all be proud."

Know your circumstances and conditions

An important part of the preparation for a negotiation is to assess the circumstances, conditions and timing of the negotiation. This can be critical in achieving success. Some questions to ask: Is it the right time to negotiate? Are there any external factors that might determine whether or when you negotiate? Are there any specific interests that you would want to be addressed that depend on other external factors?

The age old Chinese military treatise, Sun Zi *Bing Fa* a.k.a. Sun Tzu *Art of War* has highlighted the need to understand the weather and terrain in a war, which in negotiation terms translates to understanding the underlying circumstances of the negotiation, the market, the regulations, and the other external factors that have a role in the negotiations. While some of these are not necessarily under the control of the parties, they need to be closely monitored and considered in making a decision.

Deriving anchors

In the case of a negotiation that involves a quantitative or milestone aspect (such as a price, volume, due date, etc.), the starting position is called the anchor that determines the course of action for the rest of the negotiation. For example, where the parties are negotiating on a price point, the initial price quoted by each party is their anchor. A buyer quotes an anchor price with the expectation that the final price paid after one or more rounds of adjustment upwards is not significantly higher than the anchor. A seller quotes an anchor price, expecting the final selling price to be close to the anchor price after any adjustments. The objective is to derive the response based on perceived levels created by the anchors.

When and how do you derive your anchor?
At the stage of assessing interests, one of the primary objectives is to derive your anchors. These anchors need to be determined and arrived at keeping in mind the justifiable criteria that support the

anchor such as the quantifiable facts and circumstances, proper research, available prior outcomes - assuming all conditions are the same, etc.

Often, anchors are not substantiated and appear to be picked out of thin air. If the other party seeks to validate the basis of the anchor, the lack of appropriate criteria can result in a dilution of trust or questioning the authority of the party that provides the anchor. There are hardball tactics—such as lowball or highball—that people use to divert attention. Lowball refers to an anchor that is significantly lower than expected (typically used by a buyer) and highball refers to a significantly high anchor (typically used by a seller). These hardball tactics are prone to risk, as they could lead to loss of trust and failure in the negotiation. Beware of the impact of these tactics on negotiation decisions.

Realistic Anchors
A key to arriving at a beneficial anchor is that it should be realistic. So, what is a realistic anchor? It is the most appropriate anchor based on the circumstances. For example, most prospective employers ask for an expected salary. They are seeking to use that as an anchor. They expect that the candidate will state an anchor based on their current salary. However, as a candidate, one needs to be aware of the competitive market pay as the appropriate anchor. This is important, because the current salary might not be representative of the market rates. It is common understanding that the rate of salary growth while employed in an organization is slow over the years. So, if one has been employed in the same company for ten years, they would have joined at the market rate at that time ten years ago and experienced a slower growth in salary over the years; whereas, the market growth would have been significantly higher over the period of ten years. So, it would be beneficial to use a market rate as the anchor, rather than the current salary.

• • •

Assess alternatives

We have covered some important topics in the Prepare phase of a negotiation. So let's introduce a couple of new concepts. This section is to discuss reservation price and alternatives.

Reservation price

In a negotiation that involves an amount, whether it is a price, fees, salary or others, the concept of "reservation price" comes into effect. This is your base decision point.

Does it drive a decision in a negotiation?

In most cases, the reservation price will protect against making a bad decision. The one valuable decision that it might drive is whether to walk away. However, it is not the only consideration and cannot be the primary criteria to rely on.

So how important is the reservation price?

It is a checkpoint and is essential to be aware of, but a good negotiation is above and beyond the reservation price. We will discuss more on reservation price when we discuss alternatives next.

Alternatives and TRAIN

The next concept relates to alternatives. While the reservation price provides a base point, it is likely that the negotiation might not be effective, even if the reservation price is achieved. Additionally, there are circumstances where the negotiation does not go as anticipated. In such cases, it is critical that one is able to plan ahead by assessing alternatives which will be the backup option for an inconclusive negotiation.

One engages in a negotiation to achieve specific objectives. However, it is not certain that the negotiation goes as per plan. Here are some of the benefits of developing strong alternatives in a negotiation:

- Careful analysis of alternatives offers the peace of mind of an option to fall back on.
- Strong alternatives provide the leverage to negotiate with confidence.
- Developing alternatives reduces an element of uncertainty and desperation that leads to a hasty or forced decision.
- Inadequate or no alternatives could also make one anxious, irrational or defensive.

Let's look at a couple of simple examples to explain the concept of alternatives:

Example A - If you are negotiating to sell a large piece of commercial land, some of the alternatives could be to build a warehouse for leasing or lease it for a parking space or just keep it for future use.

Example B - If you are applying for a job, some of the alternatives would be to stay in the current job, go back to school or take a sabbatical and travel, take up freelance consulting, or take your favorite classes.

The process of assessing alternatives is vital to determine the alternatives that provide the most leverage. This process includes:
1. Listing all the available alternatives. It might be important to list even the options that might seem small, because it might be possible to combine a couple of options to form a significant alternative.

2. Ranking them in terms of effectiveness and likelihood of implementation.
3. Determining the most effective alternative.

As you start to evaluate the alternatives, rank them in order for alternatives that you will most benefit from and are most likely to implement. In this process, consider all available criteria that will provide the answer, such as financial implications, effectiveness, market information, ease of implementation, etc. The alternatives that result in the highest ranking based on the criteria might be the most viable alternative to fall back on if the negotiation is not conclusive. This highest ranking, most effective alternative can be referred to as **TRAIN (Top Ranked Alternative in Negotiation)**.

In **Example A** above, if you are trying to sell a piece of land and have listed the alternatives, the cost of building on the land might be prohibitive and high ownership costs make it financially impractical to keep the land for future use. However, based on market information, you might note that the demand for parking space is high, due to events and activities in the vicinity. In that case, an immediate benefit is derived from leasing the land as a parking lot, and this will be the TRAIN.

In **Example B** above, if you are applying for a job, evaluate the alternatives that you have listed. While staying in the current job might be an option, you might consider pursuing a cherished dream of going to business school or taking a sabbatical to travel. A combination of alternatives might also result in a feasible option, such as staying in the current job but agreeing to pursue a part-time MBA using an education reimbursement program. Based on the current situation, the alternatives that matter most will be ranked at the top and designated as the TRAIN.

While the foremost consideration prior to entering a negotiation discussion is to assess your own alternatives, a relatively vital action is to find out the other party's alternatives. In the prepare phase, available information can be used to analyze what could be the other party's alternatives. How likely you will be able to understand the alternatives depends on how well you know the other party and the circumstances of negotiation. In the Engage phase, we will discuss how to build on the understanding of their alternatives.

Four Quadrant Model

```
                    ▲
                    │
        ┌───────────┼───────────┐
   HIGH │           │     ★     │
        │   TRAIN   │  BEST DEAL│
        │           │           │
Impact  ├───────────┼───────────┤──▶
of result           │           │
        │  No deal  │Reservation│
   LOW  │           │   price   │
        └───────────┼───────────┘
                    │
          NO SUCCESS    SUCCESS
           Success of negotiation
```

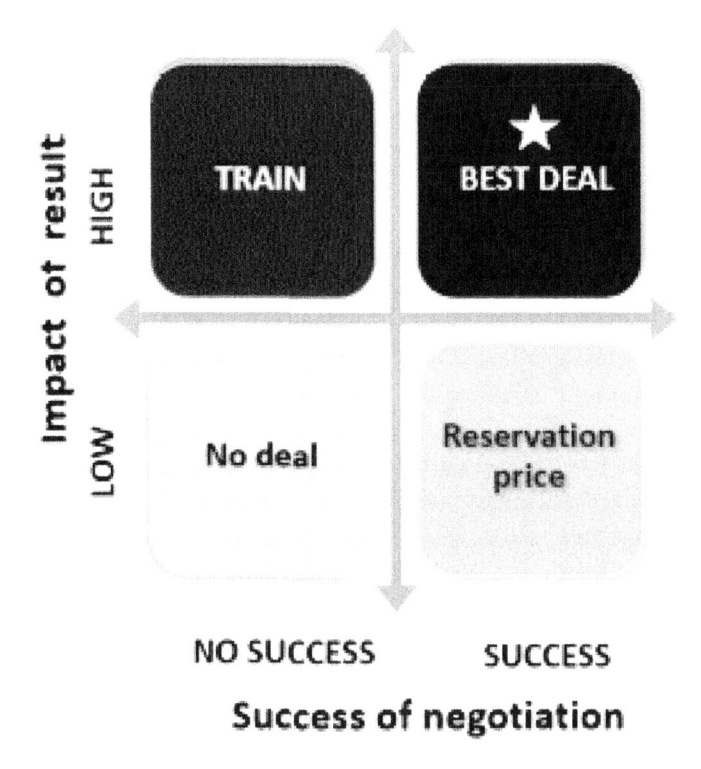

In the visual above, I have used the four quadrant model to demonstrate two primary criteria 1) impact of the accomplished result in a negotiation and 2) success of the negotiation efforts.

Let's look at these four quadrants:
- **No Deal** refers to a failed negotiation with no established TRAIN. This is low in terms of the impact of the result, as well as the no success in negotiation.
- **Reservation price** refers to a scenario where the deal is made to settle with the reservation price. This is low in the impact of the negotiation, because you could always strive to achieve much more than the reservation price, but it is a successful negotiation effort since a deal was reached.
- **TRAIN** refers to the scenario in a negotiation where no deal was reached, but a strong TRAIN exists. In this case, there is no success in the negotiation effort, but impact is high because TRAIN was selected.
- **Best Deal** is the quadrant where there is a high impact of the deal and success of negotiation efforts. This is the scenario where the final outcome was significantly better than the reservation price and the TRAIN.

One of my workshop participants separately mentioned to me an interesting story on how the TRAIN becomes significant. The story starts with the introduction of a new manager to lead the team. The participant and the new manager started off with building a relationship. They regularly met and discussed projects, as well as matters outside of work. The participant mentioned that she believed things were going in the right direction. As she admitted, one big error that she made was that she did not document the discussions. In a few months, when it came time to do performance assessments, the participant got a rude shock when she heard that her performance was not up to expectations. At this point, without adequate documentation of her performance and agreement with the manager over the months, her TRAIN was weak, and the negotiation would be difficult. She could have avoided this position if she had the facts written down and regularly agreed with the manager. This is also an important learning when one is dealing with a new negotiating party without any established relationship. It is critical in these situations to confirm understanding at every stage of the negotiation, including adequate documentation to rely on when it is most required.

A story commonly used in negotiation discussions for exploring options when the alternatives are weak comes from Teddy Roosevelt's presidential campaign. As a part of the campaign for the presidency, Roosevelt's team printed three million copies of a pamphlet with Roosevelt's photo and speech. However, before distributing these pamphlets, they noted a huge error. They realized that the photo used on the pamphlet had a copyright owned by the photography studio. As the pamphlets had already been printed, it would be a loss to discard them. At the same time, the campaign did not have enough funds to pay for the copyright and did not want to be liable for legal damages. The campaign had no meaningful alternatives. The campaign manager contacted the studio with the following cable:

"We are planning to distribute millions of pamphlets with Roosevelt's picture on the cover. It will be great publicity for the studio whose photograph we use. How much will you pay us to use yours? Respond immediately."

The studio replied with an offer to pay $250 to use the photograph.

If the campaign had referred to their TRAIN, they would have been very defensive or would have made a rash decision to lose big amounts of money. However, looking at this from the photographer's perspective, unless he knew that the pamphlets had already been printed, he did not have any strong alternatives either and would have lost an opportunity for great publicity.

In the cable message sent to the photographer, Roosevelt's campaign manager built the technique of loss anxiety (covered in Chapter 7) by adding "respond immediately" to elicit a quick decision and not provide any extra time to think or research options.

Let's look at another case of medical service providers who regularly negotiate with insurance companies for increase in insurance claim rates reimbursement, i.e., the amount that the insurance company pays the medical providers. Larger hospitals have the advantage of getting direct attention from insurance companies in the negotiation for the claim rates. Independent physicians have to work harder in this scenario. In general, while negotiating for the claim rates, the independent physicians or smaller clinics commence discussion with the agent level staff at the insurance companies. In discussions with an independent physician, I learned that the insurance agents start with an increase of three percent. The physicians start negotiating for claim rates upward from this basic increase of three percent. So the TRAIN for the independent physician is three percent. To further their chances in the negotiation for higher claim rates, the physicians need to build a much stronger case by studying the market, carrying out competitor analysis, highlighting ease of patient bookings and accessibility, demonstrating referral ecosystem, and providing an outlook of increased future claims. The process takes longer as the independent physicians must plow through the various levels of insurance staff to reach the decision maker.

Psychological alternative and TRAIN
I now introduce an interesting concept called the "psychological alternative". When a negotiation involves an alternative that does not actually exist but is only a subconscious existence of a viable alternative, it is called the psychological alternative. This psychological alternative might also become the TRAIN. Let's look at this with an example.

A colleague received a job offer at Company X and was going through final compensation negotiation. As she was finalizing her negotiation, she was informed of a couple more opportunities. She had some preliminary discussions with these new companies. While these were not actual offers on hand and should not have had much effect on my colleague's negotiation for the job offer on hand, they did play an important part as psychological alternatives. They gave her the courage to ask for sign-on bonus in her current negotiation.

One should pay attention when a decision is being made based on a psychological alternative. It might provide a boost in some circumstances, as it did to my colleague, but specific consideration needs to be given about the realistic conversion potential of the psychological alternative into an actual alternative.

The concept of alternatives has also been discussed by two stalwarts of negotiation, Prof. Roger Fisher and Prof. William Ury, in their book *Getting to Yes*, and they coined the term BATNA (Best Alternative To a Negotiated Agreement) which has been highly used in negotiation circles.

• • •

Assess types and modes of negotiations

We have reviewed the approaches to negotiation, and the framework and strategies used in preparation for a negotiation so far in this chapter. We will conclude the Prepare phase with an understanding of the distinct types and modes of negotiation. The dynamics and extent of negotiation efforts vary, depending on the type and mode of negotiation, and proper planning and consideration to address these criteria become vital as you enter a negotiation.

In any case, whichever type and mode of negotiation applies, it is useful to prepare with mock exercises or simulations. Keeping in mind the various scenarios that could come up and working out a plan for those will provide a strong platform for success. Ever wondered how some teams who you interact or negotiate with are so well-coordinated? This is the importance of proper practice and alignment of roles and tasks.

Types of negotiation
Let's review the various types of negotiation.

Two-party
These are the most common negotiations that we all encounter on a daily basis. This type of negotiation involves two parties negotiating to meet their objectives and might be either the distributive or integrative negotiation. The parties may be two individuals or two groups of people. The duration of these negotiations also varies. Sometimes, these negotiations last for a few minutes and sometimes, these can last for months. A key aspect of these negotiations is the identification of the strategy, as well as appropriate behaviors and techniques that apply to these negotiations.

Note that a two-party negotiation might be between two groups. In this case, alignment within the group is vital. Proper understanding of interests and styles of all the group members becomes crucial.

A couple of examples highlight the varying degrees of these types of negotiations.

Often, just one conversation can have a deep impact in a negotiation. A participant at a leadership seminar narrated a story of a classic two-party negotiation. This was his negotiation with his manager. The manager asked him to research a new technology that would replace the existing technology. The participant was negotiating for time to complete the research. His take was that he had other activities that took priority over the research of the new technology.

One day, the manager invited the participant to join him on the way to a customer's site and discuss further. The manager noted that the research had not moved as far ahead as he had anticipated. In the negotiation to prioritize the research, the manager used two key strategies. The first strategy was the use of the "Bonding" technique (discussed further in Chapter 7). He told the participant that of all the people on the team, he believed in the participant to get the work done. This was effective in building trust. The second strategy that the manager brought up was the use of "Vividness" to highlight the consequence of not evaluating the new software. As the new software brings efficiency, it would help to significantly reduce costs. This will also enable the organization to channel resources to accomplish other important projects in the pipeline. If the new technology was not implemented, the only way to reduce costs was by reducing the bonus and compensation increases in the team for the current year and delays in starting important projects. Vividness in presenting the consequences helped the participant to better appreciate the urgency to evaluate the software.

An example where a negotiation could last for a long time is a case highlighted by a colleague. It is a negotiation between a senior executive and a senior manager. When the executive joined the company, he inquired about an operations model that the senior manager had put in place. The executive did not fully understand the value of the operations model and believed that it should be scrapped. However, since he was new, he heard the arguments provided and allowed for some additional time to prove that his thinking was right. The difference of opinion arose because the executive believed that the team was performing work that other teams are accountable for, but the senior manager emphasized that this model provided accuracy and efficiency. The difference of opinion grew over time as the executive became convinced that his thinking was correct. At one point, after multiple rounds of negotiation over eighteen months, the executive finally changed his stance. He argued strongly that the operations model was wrong and asked the senior manager to prove that his thinking was wrong. At last update, the negotiation continued with the senior manager gathering additional facts and analysis to explain his position.

Multi-party
As the name suggests, these negotiations involve multiple parties and the objectives of all the parties come into play. Again, these parties may be multiple individuals or multiple groups. These negotiations most frequently follow the Integrative approach. As the interests of multiple parties are involved, solutions need to address those objectives. This makes these types of negotiations generally much more difficult.

Similar to the two-party negotiation, if the multi-party negotiation is between or among groups, it is pertinent to have an internal group agreement before negotiating inter-group. Intra-group alignment is vital. Proper understanding of interests and styles of all the group members becomes crucial.

An interesting case of multi-party negotiation involves aligning objectives of the parties and leveraging relationships to achieve an objective that was seemingly difficult to accomplish by regular discussions. In this case, there are four parties involved in the negotiation with two primary parties and two parties that play an important part in influencing the decision towards achieving the negotiation objectives. The primary parties in the negotiation are the head of operations and the chief financial officer of Region D at a large corporation.

The operations team partnered with the regional finance teams to design and develop a new financial transaction management tool to record and monitor all client services transactions. This system was built with several advanced features that improved the efficiency of work and accuracy of data. It was a monumental shift from the manual effort in place for recording and monitoring the client services transactions. The objectives for the operations team were to introduce methods of faster transaction processing via automation of the process while providing accurate data. This was the right direction for the company. The head of operations was driving towards implementation of the system for client services transactions across all the regions.

The implementation was successfully completed in three regions—A, B, and C—with positive results. However, in Region D, the CFO was in two minds about using this new system. The CFO and his team appreciated all the benefits resulting from this new system, but were also apprehensive of this new system, because his region had low volumes of client services transactions. The CFO and his staff wondered if this system was beneficial for their region and if it was worth investing all the time to learn and implement this system. They debated that it would be a better use of their time to focus on other higher priority activities. However, the operations team highlighted the enhanced accuracy of the results of Region D from recording these transactions in the new system. After all, this was one of the primary reasons for the development of the system. The ease of use of the new system and the consistency of the process around the globe were the additional criteria supporting the adoption of the new system. However, the finance team of Region D continued to push back due to the lower volume of these transactions than the other three regions. The operations team faced major challenges in their negotiation to implement this system in Region D.

While the operations team and the Region D teams continued their negotiation regarding the adoption of the new system, the head of operations partnered with the head of procurement in an interesting way. They both had established a good working relationship. The operations team demonstrated the features of the new system to the head of procurement. In these discussions, a surprise element was uncovered. The head of procurement asked if this system could be used for the company's government services transactions. The head of procurement and the head of operations agreed that these government services transactions are similar to client services. As a result, the operations team demonstrated this tool to the head of government services, who was very impressed with the tool. Government services transactions were lacking a proper tracking system, and this tool provided the ability to monitor the transactions. The operations team influenced the head of government services to utilize the functionality of the system. This support was a crucial turning point, and the head of operations now had the ammunition to negotiate strongly with the CFO of Region D to adopt the tool for the government services transactions.

It was noted that the government services transactions were primarily applicable only in Region D and were not managed by the finance teams in the other regions. Region D had a big volume of these government transactions and this became a key criterion in the negotiation for implementation of the new system. The CFO was now presented with a revised business case for the use of the new system that resulted in improved efficiencies, provided accurate results, and was easy to use for the finance team of Region D to track the government services transactions, along with their client services transactions. This clinched the deal for the operations team!

Mediation
This is another very common negotiation. It is frequently used in case of disputes or differences of opinion. In the case of conflicts, some common methods of negotiation are mediation and arbitration. If these methods do not work, the final option is to go to court. A mediator is brought in such cases to help resolve the

differences between the two parties and plays a very important role in the negotiation between the two parties. In the case of mediation, there is a high likelihood of parties accepting a compromise, as the mediator wants the fair chance for both parties.

This is different from arbitration, where an arbitrator listens to both sides and makes a decision that is binding on both. Arbitration is similar to a lawsuit but it happens outside the courts.

A typical case of mediation in daily life is illustrated from a story. During a family drive, a mother mentioned that a friend was getting a fish tank. Within a few minutes, the 12-year-old daughter started crying at the back seat in the car. Wondering what suddenly happened to her, the parents asked why she was crying, and she was hesitant to say anything. They assumed it was because of the videos she was watching on her phone and instructed her to stop watching the videos. At this point, the daughter revealed she was crying because she felt that she would never get a pet.

Concerned about the incident, dad asked daughter the next day, "Why did you start crying yesterday?" Dad wanted to ensure that the daughter was able to articulate the concerns, so that they could be addressed adequately.

The daughter said, "Whenever I ask for a pet, Mom declines. I now think that I will never be able to get a pet."

At this, the dad asked, "Have you ever thought why mom refuses to get a pet? Do you know how much more work there is in caring for a pet?"

"I can do all the work and take care of the pet," the daughter said. At this comment, the dad explained, "If you want to convince Mom, you will need to show that you are responsible for the next three months by attending to all your daily activities quickly and helping with household chores. If you could do that, mom might think about getting a pet." At the same time, they discussed what kind of pet the daughter would like to have and agreed that a small pet, such as a hamster, might be easier to take care of and would make her responsible.

At the same time, Dad separately discussed it with Mom and expressed that it was not good for the daughter to get so emotional about the pet. He explained that the daughter was getting more responsible and was willing to help with more chores, so it might be time to get a small pet. Furthermore, this might help to keep the younger daughter engaged and responsible, too. The mom understood that a small pet is much less work and her interests were also to keep both the daughters happy. They agreed to get a pet in the next three months.

Coalition

An alliance of multiple parties to join forces in a negotiation is called a coalition. The parties that join a coalition are aligned on their common objectives. Such a coalition provides the strength of numbers in a negotiation. Parties get into coalition so that it gives them the leverage to negotiate better. In many cases, multiple smaller or weaker parties join together to negotiate against a stronger party. The analysis of the multiple issues of the parties in the coalition becomes vital in developing strategies for the negotiation in the Prepare phase, as well as during the negotiation engagement. In general, coalitions are considered more unstable, due to the fact that multiple parties form the coalition.

In a discussion with a friend, I heard a story on how a coalition can drive positive results in a negotiation. He mentioned a successful negotiation for a group of parents with a school.

At a roadshow during an education expo event, a couple of parents came to the booth of a new school. In a city where school fees form a substantial cost for a family, having an alternative sparked an interest in the parents. They inquired with the representatives of the school and learned that the fee was $14,000 per year. The parents proposed to bring in numbers if the fees could be reduced, and the representatives of the school agreed to discuss this with their management. The meeting ended there with a possibility of a new beginning for many children.

The parents harnessed the power of technology to create a coalition, and one couple emerged as the leader of this coalition. The couple sent messages about the new school to some groups on WhatsApp, and within two days, a dozen parents had signed up. They also created Google Docs to prepare a list of all interested parents. As the number of families grew to reach about 50 over the next few days, they pushed forward on the fee negotiation, and the school management came back with an offer of $10,800, a 23 percent reduction in fees. Parents were invited to a meeting at the school where they could discuss with the management and gather additional information.

As word reached all corners, the numbers kept swelling, and at one point, there were over 100 families willing to attend the meeting at the school. The school was overwhelmed by the response and scheduled a couple of sessions with the parents. The management clearly saw this as an important deal. The parents were willing to move their kids to this new school, as they had been subjected to annual increases in school fees of ten percent or higher at the current schools. Parents were fully aware that they had a strong coalition, and this was a highly rewarding deal for the school, so they even negotiated a freeze in fees for three years. Apart from the school tuition, transport is generally a big cost to the parents and serves as an additional criterion for the parents to negotiate. They managed to get favorable results on that front, too. For the school, this was a long-term commitment that they were happy to enter into.

Happy parents and eager students turned out to be the right formula for the school to establish itself. All in all, this was a big win-win for the coalition and the school.

Agent
In many situations, the parties choose not to or are not permitted to negotiate with each other directly. In these cases, they negotiate via an agent. An agent is the custodian who negotiates a deal on behalf of the principal. The agent has to accomplish the objectives of the principal. A negotiation with agents could apply to a two-party or a multi-party negotiation.

It is important that the agent understands and pursues the interests of the principal in the negotiation. The agent should not have conflicting interests that will prevent them from making the best decision. For example, if the agent's compensation is based on getting a deal done, they might settle with the reservation price and not want to fall back on the TRAIN, as it impacts their compensation. This might not achieve the best interests of the principal, who might prefer to opt for the TRAIN. The value of an agent is when they go beyond the basic idea of closing a deal to accomplishing an impactful negotiation, keeping in mind all the interests of the principal.

The relationship between the principal and the agent needs to be strong, so that they both understand the interests of each other. As the agent is interacting with the other party, sometimes, they might have to make a quick decision. The agent should be aware of all the requirements of the principal. Further, the principal needs to provide specific instructions to the agent for the circumstances where the agent will need to make a compromise. This will help them plan for the negotiation with the highest impact.

In some cases, the agent represents both parties. This is a tricky situation, as it might be difficult for the same agent to attend to the interests of both parties. For example, in a property transaction, often an agent represents both the seller and the buyer in the same transaction. In such cases, it is inevitable that the interests of one of the parties will be compromised.

Click-Thru Negotiation
Last but certainly not least, is a type of negotiation that is picking up a lot of steam in the last few years. I call this "Click-thru negotiation", due to the primary nature of these negotiations happening without any direct interactions between the parties. These "intuitive negotiations" are happening online between a user on one side and the algorithm on the other side.

How many of us book travel online these days? Almost everybody. A significant part of the online booking experience highlights the essence of click-thru negotiation. With the ascent of the internet, this kind of negotiation has flourished. So, when you book air travel online, you express your interests, such as time of the day for travel, number of stops, price range, and such choices made during the booking. You are presented with multiple options to book airfare with different carriers, at different times and via different routes. Every option results in different fares. Based on changes in your interests, the options generated in this intuitive negotiation vary. There are multiple solutions offered by the portal that build on interests and help to "grow the pie". The travel portal also bundles services as a "travel package" where the airfare can be combined with hotel and car rental to list better options. The travel portal is using subtle negotiation/influencing tactics by listing different options in the algorithm. We discuss influencing techniques in more detail in Chapter 7, but the travel portal is applying most of the techniques to influence your decision. You are an integral part of this negotiation, as you are driving the decisions via the "click-thru" experience.

Similarly, online shopping is another common example of the "click-thru" negotiation. Let's look at Amazon to understand this further. Amazon does not negotiate directly with users, but has incorporated a similar "click-thru" approach as a part of the overall shopping experience. Shoppers search for the item they intend to research and buy. The portal checks for their interests - such as price range, choice between new or used items, etc. - and then generates multiple options. To add value, the shoppers are shown additional items that can be bundled with the item that the shopper is buying. Amazon provides the references in the form of ratings and reviews to further help in decision-making. Amazon's subscription plan is a "click-thru" negotiation experience that seeks to "grow the pie" and induce commitment from the buyers. Amazon offers the option of buying some items that users buy frequently on a subscription plan with discounted prices, rather than a one-time purchase. Additional discounts are available for multiple items subscribed. The users can also pick a schedule for subscription or defer schedule with just a click of a button.

Modes of negotiation

There are several modes to carry out a negotiation. It is critical to know which would work the best depending on the scenario and circumstances. In general, the following are the different modes of undergoing the negotiation discussions:

1. In-person or live negotiation
2. Remote negotiation

The question I am often asked is which mode is the best in a negotiation. The answer in my mind, of course, is in-person or live negotiation. The interactions conducted live where it is possible to see each other and read body language and expressions closely help in building the connection. Eye contact helps to develop a strong connection. If possible, in person attendance is preferable as it also demonstrates the efforts taken to positively push forward the negotiations.

This is illustrated in a story from *The Google Story*, by David A. Vise and Mark Malseed. Here's an excerpt of this riveting story:

In 2004, Google founders Larry Page and Sergey Brin were flying to Spain when they received a call from their sales head, Omid Kordestani, that AOL was going to award the European ad provider contract to Yahoo's Overture. Sergey was not ready to accept this defeat. If Yahoo could offer a better deal, so could Google. Sergey asked Khordestani to immediately inform Philip Rowley, head of AOL Europe, that Larry and Sergey were on their way to London to meet him in person immediately. When he was notified by Kordestani that AOL had already struck a deal with Yahoo, Sergey persisted that Google would be able to build much better terms and sent a message to ask Rowley to hold off on finalizing the deal with Yahoo until he hears directly from them. Rowley and Jon Miller, CEO of AOL, discussed and agreed to meet Google. This was a big step in the negotiation, as the doors would now potentially open for a deal. The idea of meeting Google executives, who were interested in meeting in person to put a lucrative deal on the table, provided sufficient influence. They were eager to hear what Google had in mind. For Google, getting AOL's Europe business was a significant interest, and they knew that an extraordinary offer would clinch the deal. Google clearly identified the growth in the Internet, and especially in the international markets, which were growing faster than the mature U.S. markets, and believed that this was the time to participate via an offer that would prove to be a long-term growth driver. They lured AOL with a very attractive proposal with financial guarantees for a multi-year deal that AOL could not resist. AOL's business had been running ads from Overture since January 2002, and Yahoo's Overture finally ceded to Google.

Google founders demonstrated commitment by traveling to London and asking for a chance to be heard and by wanting to meet Rowley immediately. When Rowley mentioned this to Miller in the U.S., they agreed to reciprocate by agreeing to hold off with Yahoo until they had heard from Google. Due to the nature of this negotiation, it was critical for Larry and Sergey to build the level of commitment and urgency. They further emphasized the importance of the deal to Google by staying back in London until the contract was finalized. Yahoo had been given the opportunity to make a counteroffer in response to Google's offer, but they were overconfident and did not want to take part in a competitive bidding experience. It was an unfavorable result for Yahoo and showed the character of a company that did not anticipate a tough negotiation and were not prepared for such a situation.

The presence of the founders in London was an important behavior that was vital in this deal. As Rowley clearly stated, this was a big difference in signing the deal with Google. Their quick decision-making and persistence helped them to get a chance before the deal was finalized with Yahoo. By being in London, Larry and Sergey helped to build the trust and the bonding with Rowley that proved to be critical for building a long-term relationship. As Rowley mentioned, "They were pretty laid-back and cool. I wanted to do business with these guys. If they hadn't been there, this would never have happened" (*The Google Story*, 2005, Page 207).

When you decide to have an in-person meeting, pay attention to the location and setting also. Another important factor is the number of team members you bring to the negotiation and how it would match the other side. These factors gain utmost importance when you are negotiating with a person from a different culture where these factors are critical.

In this age of advanced technology, negotiations are often carried out remotely. Use of video technology is the next best to having face-to-face negotiations and is particularly helpful in those scenarios where the other person is in another location and it is not easy to meet in person. Remote negotiations on phone or email need strong verbal or written communication skills as the other party cannot see body language or expressions. All types of negotiations mentioned above could be carried out face-to-face or remotely. Since 2020, this mode of communication has been forced on us due to the pandemic. Here are some aspects to consider for remote negotiations.

Video is better than phone or email - The next best to an in-person negotiation is a video negotiation. Use of technologies for video conferencing such as Zoom, Skype, Webex etc. will enable you to at least see the other person and observe their expressions. Ensure the technology works seamlessly. Messaging or chat applications are the least preferred mode of professional negotiations in my opinion. They are prone to misunderstanding and confusion.

Focus on communication essentials - It's important to focus on attentive listening and clear articulation of all points. Use effective communication skills such as asking open ended conversations, repeating or rephrasing what you heard to avoid any misunderstanding, and proper conclusion of all agreed points. The video environment should facilitate proper communication.

Alignment within the group - If you are in a group to group negotiation, ensure you have completed your intra-group alignments via video conferencing and have agreed on all negotiation points within the group, before going into the negotiation with the other group. If multiple people are in a negotiation, ensure that the exchanges and conversations are clearly understood.

Document everything - Properly document the negotiation objectives in advance and the meeting discussions. If it is acceptable to all participants, record the meeting. An email to follow up discussions is crucial. Do this immediately after so that the discussions are still fresh in the mind.

Focus on appropriate behaviors - Appropriate behaviors such as respect, flexibility, ethics etc. are as important in remote negotiations as in face-to-face negotiations. Minimize distractions during the engagement to focus on the person on the video. Never escalate conflicts in remote negotiations as they are not likely to end well.

• • •

Summary

This chapter discussed the aspects that laid the foundation for a successful negotiation. In this chapter, we reviewed the approaches to, and types and modes of negotiations, understood the importance of assessing interests and alternatives, and examined the CAV Framework. These concepts help to prepare effectively to be able to put the best foot forward in the negotiation. The checklist in Appendix B acts as a guide for the key steps to note during the Prepare phase.

CHAPTER 4
Engage

Interaction

As we move from the Prepare phase to the Engage phase, the efforts of preparation are put to practice in the actual interaction with the other party or parties. Success of the negotiation depends as much on the interaction in the Engage phase as it does on the preparation. In many cases, the Engage phase is far more critical than the preparation. Dynamics of the negotiation can change, depending on the interaction with the negotiating party. Some of the key considerations in the interaction are below.

1) Build on Interests and devising solutions

The Engage phase provides the opportunity to build further on the interests. In the Prepare phase, we have described the importance of assessing interests, but in our discussions with the other party we can further add to our knowledge of the other party's interests. There are a few ways to do this:

- Interact with the negotiating party and unveil their priorities.
- Confirm that your assessment of their interests still align with the other party's priorities.
- Convert positions to interests by listening carefully and asking open-ended questions.

This is valuable in our negotiations as the proper assessment of our and their interests will result in building creative solutions. This is what will drive the negotiations forward toward success.

Imagine how you would react if you heard that the global e-commerce and technology leader Amazon received their approval in just 11 days to build a massive office premises in Hyderabad in the Telangana state of India. This was Amazon's largest state-of-the-art campus in the world. There must be clear win-win solutions to accomplish such a quick deal. Generally, approvals for such large projects could take months, if not years.

The Telangana authorities promoted their online self-certification service, which enabled Amazon to apply for all the certification online and receive quick approvals. The process is advertised as simple and transparent. All documents are uploaded online, eliminating the handling of documents. For the authorities, it was important to promote the benefits and make it a success for companies to use the service. There would not be a better way to spotlight the easy self-certification service than getting it right for a global giant such as Amazon. During the Engage phase, the authorities elaborated on three additional interests in this process:

1. Marketing support for the textile industry and weavers in the state via Amazon's platform;
2. Assisting the city to improve the artificial intelligence focus; and
3. Partnering with the city to increase its corporate social responsibility efforts.

For Amazon, using the online self-certification and obtaining quick approvals was of primary interest, but at the same time they wanted to build a long-term relationship with the State of Telangana by helping the authorities to promote the online self-certification service and addressing the three additional interests that the authorities brought to the table. During the Engage phase, Amazon also managed to receive some exemptions from the requirements in the application and construction process.

A vital step in building on the interests of the other party is to understand the key decision-maker's objectives in order to be able to attend to those objectives. This is specifically important in some cultures where the decisions are made and influenced by one individual or a group of key individuals.

A good example of building on interests emerged during discussions with a colleague, emphasizing the importance of understanding the interests of the key decision-maker and thereby creating value for both parties. A consulting firm was negotiating for services related to implementation of a new system. Several discussions were held with the consulting firm, and the negotiation was progressing in the right direction. At this point, the partner of the firm understood that the head of operations was the primary lead in driving the implementation. In a couple of meetings with the head of operations, the partner discovered that she was responsible for change management, too. The partner presented her an overview of change management services that the firm provided and also agreed to add in pro bono change management services for an upcoming workshop. This caught the attention of the head of operations, resulting in some additional change management services added to the proposal. The partner was able to develop trust and build a strong relationship with the head of operations.

2) Confirm Alternatives
At the Prepare phase, we assessed our alternatives and determined our TRAIN. From a careful analysis and review of available information, we also assessed what we believed were the other party's alternatives. Assessing alternatives were valuable for walking into the negotiation with an understanding of the back-up options if the deal did not work out.

In the Engage phase, the alternatives are further developed and confirmed. Based on the discussions, your own TRAIN might need to be revised if circumstances have changed. What's more, new information could confirm or change the evaluation of the other party's alternatives.

In the course of the interaction, there are ways to check on the other party's alternatives. It is not an easy task to find their alternatives, as they might not be forthright with the information, but asking the right questions and listening carefully can help to get some clues about their alternatives. Sometimes you can directly ask the question, and at other times you need to ask leading questions.

Let's look at some ways to find out the other party's alternatives in our examples previously discussed in the Prepare phase.

Example A
If you are a seller of the land and are trying to find out the other party's alternatives, some questions could be:
- Is this your primary location of interest?
- What is the ideal space that you need?
- We have property in X location. What are your thoughts on that location?

If you are a buyer of the land, you could ask some of the following:
- What has been your primary use for this land previously?
- What other purposes can this land be used for?
- Do you have property in other locations?

Example B
Let's assume you are the interviewer and need to find out the candidate's alternatives. Some questions to ask could include:
- What other companies are you considering?
- In which other industries are you interested?
- What interests do you actively pursue after work?
- We have a tuition reimbursement. What are your thoughts about pursuing higher education?

If you are the candidate, you might ask:
- How quickly are you looking to fill the role?
- How many candidates do you have in your pipeline?
- What is your ideal candidate like?

3) Conduct during the interaction

The final critical component of the interaction is the conduct in the discussions. We will discuss the valuable behaviors, such as gaining trust and credibility, effective communication, and focus on emotions and body language that impact negotiations in detail in Chapter 6. However, certain key attributes for consideration regarding the conduct are mentioned below.

Spontaneity
Spontaneity is an important attribute that provides valuable leverage in negotiations. We can also refer to this as proactiveness. It helps with quick decision-making and reacting appropriately to circumstances and developments in a discussion. Proper preparation and practice will help facilitate a positive engagement with the other party.

Courage to ask
An important consideration as part of the communication is to have the courage to ask. In many cases, we hold back our views due to the fear of asking for too much. While the mind considers something an excessive request and fears being declined, the

chances are higher that value will be left on the table by not mustering enough courage to speak out. A comment that a participant made during one of my workshops was that she did not have the courage to ask for a sign-on bonus while she was negotiating on her job offer. I told her that knowing how hiring managers think and work, if she has an offer on hand, it is more likely that she is the best candidate. If she realized this, she would have at least asked once about a sign-on bonus. She did not muster the courage to ask for it and missed a golden opportunity.

Persistence

Persistence is an effective aspect to consider as part of the engagement. This behavior has been questioned on its effectiveness as it can be a double-edged sword. However, in my opinion it is a significant part of negotiations. Persistence is the ability to push on toward achieving an objective through continuous engagement and communication. Even if the result derived from persisting is not exactly as originally intended, at least a result is generated, which is better than having no result at all. Some people might view persistence as an inconvenience or as a matter of ego, but it can prove potent in many cases.

In general, kids are great proponents of this behavior when they negotiate, since they are determined not to give up. One such example was a story narrated by a friend recently. A ten-year-old once approached his dad and said, "Dad, I always have to come to you and trouble you for the password for downloading a game on my iPad. Also, since you are traveling and you are busy, I cannot reach you and do not want to disturb you. So why don't you give me your password, and I will let you know when I am downloading the game?" A smart technique used by a little kid. He highlighted the interests of his dad while also offering to inform him after downloading the game. In this case, the dad almost fell for the strategy, but in time realized what just hit him and so he declined.

This, however, did not deter the boy who persisted by trying different ways every few weeks.

It was amusing to observe a toddler on one of my flights. I believe the toddler wanted to walk around the airplane, but the mother did not want to let him wander about. The toddler would wail for a while and then stop to look at his mom. If he did not get the anticipated response, he would start wailing again. One can never say what was going on in his mind, but if these were negotiation tactics, I believe that over time he would become an effective negotiator.

Negoptimism
Well, is this a word? I coined this term to represent the significance that a positive attitude can have on any negotiation interactions. The mindset at the beginning and during the discussions need to be unbiased. Any prior information about the negotiation counter-party should be positively approached and biased opinions should be set aside. A positive frame of mind produces better results.

In Chapter 2, I covered the story of Google founders negotiating with AOL. One of the primary lessons from that story is the relevance of negoptimism. Sergey Brin just refused to give up because he was optimistic that they would succeed in the negotiation.

Framing
Framing is the ability to present options in a manner that elicits an anticipated reaction from the other party. Often, it is important to be able to frame a conversation or a proposal such that it registers as a beneficial choice and provides the good vibes to them.

It is well-known that any discussion is fruitful if the other party gets a positive feeling. This also applies to negotiations. The ability to frame a negotiation discussion as a positive outcome to the other party will generate better results. They are likely to be more welcoming of proposals and collaborate on options. So, while addressing the counter-party's interests is one vital aspect, clearly articulating the benefits and gains to generate the positive feeling will help to steer the discussion in a favorable direction. Another way to highlight the positive aspects is by showing how you could help address the negative outcomes if the other party does not follow an anticipated route that is the subject of the negotiation. This leads them to believe in the positive aspects of the item under discussion.

Conversely, if the other party perceives any risk in the negotiation discussions, it is likely that they will be reluctant to make any decisions or create solutions. They will be on the back foot if they do not fully develop trust and are likely to push back on the options provided to them. Uncertainty is also a cause for apprehension and could lead to an adverse impact. Hence, any information presented needs to ensure that it brings forth the potential benefits and also eliminates uncertainty.

Here's a case on how effective use of framing can help tackle a difficult situation. I have been impressed by the story of Tom Perkins (Thomas J. Perkins, businessman venture capitalist and founder of venture firm Kleiner Perkins) since I first attended his talk during his visit to Google headquarters. His talk was captivating and prompted me to learn more about him from his book *The Valley Boy*. In the book, Tom narrated several occasions when he had to use strong negotiation skills and influencing abilities. One such interesting story was from his early career when he joined HP and started working in the sales department. In those days, the company did not have a sales force and had to work with external sales representative organizations. Tom worked with Mr. Norm Neely, owner of Neely Enterprises, an established sales organization. As a young MBA in the organization, Tom knew that it would be very difficult for him to supervise Mr. Neely and his team without building enough credibility. Credibility and trust is built over time through a series of actions. It was also a time when the external sales representatives sensed that HP might develop their own internal sales department. This added complexity to Tom's role. He sensed this before his first meeting with Mr. Neely and recognized that he had to keep Mr. Neely's interests in mind. He developed an important strategy to deal with this situation. Instead of instructing Mr. Neely, Tom's idea was to present himself as their contact to get things done within HP. Indeed, his idea was a smart way to frame this and build the trust that helped him to deliver his messages to external sales representatives.

Framing is specifically important to derive a favorable outcome when people play the role of a coordinator amongst several stakeholders. In our corporate world, let's take the example of a project manager who has to interact with several stakeholders during the course of regular business. In this project management role, it is important to frame the negotiation towards positive aspects for all parties. In many cases, if it is not possible to highlight a positive or a benefit for some parties, it is important to clearly articulate and justify the "bad news" or soften the message with positives, if any. Often, the benefit to the whole company is the overarching positive that the project manager can call out for all the parties; thus, the whole is greater than the sum of the parts.

Bruce Lee, in his early career, was approached to open and run a nationwide chain of Kung Fu schools to teach teens and young adults. Financially, it would have been the right move for his career. However, it did not align with his philosophy. He did not want to "commoditize" his skills. Lee had a clever strategy to promote his art. Instead of the classes for teens and young adults, he framed it as private lessons for high-end celebrity clients. Lee decided to charge $25 per hour, a substantial charge in those days. However, initially there was no interest in Bruce Lee or his Kung Fu lessons.

Lee met Charles Fitzsimons, the co-producer of the TV show *Green Hornet*, in which Bruce Lee starred as the character Kato. Fitzsimons also gave Lee the same idea to teach celebrities Kung Fu. When Lee mentioned that he had already thought about that but there was no interest, Fitzsimons asked him how much he was charging, and Lee mentioned $25 per hour. Fitzsimons told him that he had now acted on TV, so he should charge $50, and Lee was amazed. Subsequently, when Lee announced that he was offering private lessons for $500 for 10 classes, it generated a positive feeling in terms of its value and appeal, and it didn't take long before clients started signing up. The framing as high-end private lessons from TV star Kato immediately got the results.

Framing can play an important role in negotiations when your service is closely similar to service offered by other providers. In one of my discussions with a friend in the travel industry providing B2B services to organizations, I asked what their USP was in their discussions with customers to provide travel booking services. As the travel booking industry was highly competitive, this question was intended to understand what the key points in their negotiations were with the corporate customers. He highlighted that they provide superior technology-focused services with powerful data-mining capabilities. They are able to create the same experience on the desktop, as well as on mobile. Anybody booking travel services can instantly switch from desktop to mobile. In addition, he also emphasized that they are able to generate timely reporting to match the requirements of the customers. I was curious to find out more since these are now standard services for most travel providers. He was excited about the exceptional service they are able to offer directly to the employees of their customers based on the available data. So, the B2B (Business to Business) service becomes B2B2E (Business to Business to Employee). For example, if an employee is traveling back on a Saturday morning and there is another cheaper option available for Friday night, the system is able to let the employee know directly of the availability of a cheaper flight, in case they want to change the flight. Similarly, if any emergencies are expected during the travel, the employee can immediately be informed by the algorithm. Framing the discussions to showcase several benefits brings out the positives that the customers are likely to appreciate.

Framing can be understood in a different way when it comes to kids. Since the intent of framing is to create a positive feeling in the other party, when it comes to engaging with kids, gamification of the process will be helpful to create that feeling and to appear beneficial. So in case of any discussion with kids and young adults, it will be useful to gamify the topic. As an example, if you are negotiating with the kids to help with chores, it is important to make the chore appear as fun via gamification and thereby result in positive feeling.

"Perceptual Contrast" effect:
The first time I read about perceptual contrast was in *Influence: Science and Practice* by Dr. Robert Cialdini. It resonated with me, as many things that I have experienced or observed are linked to perceptual contrast. When two things are mentioned or shown in immediate succession, the effect of the first thing weighs heavily on the mind, resulting in an anticipated behavior towards the second thing. Often, sales staff present a high-value item first and then show a lower-value item with the objective of selling the lower-value items. Similarly, when a purchase of high-value items is made, lower-value items such as accessories are presented immediately after the purchase to induce another buying decision. In both these cases, the perceptual contrast created by the higher-value item is strong enough to drive a behavior.

To illustrate the concept of perceptual contrast let's look at a simple example from daily life. I was negotiating with my wife for karaoke apps for beginners. YouTube provided some good options and was my preferred solution as a beginner. We heard of an app called

"MeraGana" commonly used by most of our network. This was my wife's preference. The difference was that YouTube was free and commonly used by beginners, but might not be fun to use; whereas, MeraGana was more accurate, comprehensive, and a better experience. However, it came with a monthly charge or annual subscription. After negotiations, a consensus was not forthcoming. At this time, a new app called Smule was introduced in the mix. Smule app was also a good option and was more popular. Upon further review, I discovered that the subscription price for Smule was eight times the price of MeraGana for a monthly subscription. The Smule pricing immediately triggered the perceptual contrast and made the decision easier to go with the accuracy of MeraGana for a smaller charge than Smule.

Anchoring

As mentioned in the Prepare phase, when a negotiation involves a quantitative or milestone aspect, the starting position is called the anchor which determines the course in the negotiation. Anchors need to be derived during the Prepare phase based on meaningful and justifiable criteria.

What's more, while the anchor might be based on proper considerations, the Engage phase is vital in the manner in which the anchor is delivered, perceived, and how it is adjusted. Adjustments to anchors are valid in the Engage phase as you learn more about the other party's considerations. However, even the adjustment of the anchors needs to be carefully thought and planned. One important lesson on the adjustment of anchors was presented during my workshops by a senior executive of an organization. This story illustrates how the adjustment of anchors was not done well. The executive stated that when he was a consultant and was negotiating the fees with a client, he realized the importance of gradually and carefully adjusting the anchor. He started at $900,000, while the client started at a lower level. When he adjusted the anchor down to $850,000, the client moved up his offer a bit higher. His next move was intended to close the discussion, so he came down to a final price of $750,000. What he did not realize was that the final price in his mind turned out to be a big negative factor for him. This erratic adjustment downward from $850,000 to $750,000 was much bigger than the previous adjustment. At this stage, the client was not sure if $750,000 was indeed the final price or if there was scope for further reduction. He highlighted that the reduction of fees should have been lower with each new anchor to give the client the idea that there is no more scope to negotiate.

In the professional world, there are many internal negotiations that involve anchoring effects. For example, an IT manager who is working on the development of a new system will create an anchor date as the deadline for launch. In many cases, we have heard that this date includes buffer time. While it is perfectly valid to state a particular date as an anchor, the IT manager should be able to justify the dates. Another example of anchoring in the corporate world is the goal-setting exercise that involves quantitative or milestone criteria. The manager and employee both decide on the final goal after starting with their initial positions serving as anchors. In this case, both sides should be able to justify the anchors they use.

It is noteworthy that anchors are a starting point, but by no means the end of the negotiation. Negotiations can be made much more effective by growing the pie, which can be achieved by bringing in other criteria in the mix.

Additional critical points about anchors are mentioned below to complete the understanding of anchors:

Who should start with the anchor?
One of the common questions concerning anchors is who should start with their anchor. Let's look at this question from two different angles. First, when the parties have a good understanding of the

price point and market dynamics. Here, it doesn't matter who makes the first offer, since the one making a counteroffer will seek an explanation of the anchor and present a strong anchor with adequate justifiable criteria. Proper preparation is needed in this matter during the Prepare phase to determine the approach. Second, if there is no proper available information on the anchor price or if uncertainties exist about the market, it will not matter who goes first because you are not sure what the other party's reaction or counteroffer will be to the first offer. Research shows that the first offer drives the discussion, but when there is no justifiable information, the counteroffer could potentially be significantly different.

Anchor and TRAIN
Anchor has close correlation with TRAIN (discussed in Chapter 3). If Party A has a strong TRAIN, any anchors that Party B starts with would not bog down Party A. The strong TRAIN also enables Party A to have the courage to put in the first offer. However, if the TRAIN and alternatives for Party A are weak, Party B's anchor might drive the final price since Party A is vulnerable due to the weak TRAIN.

Framing with anchors
There are enhancing and diminishing factors that can drive a price higher or lower. Framing with the appropriate use of such factors helps to respond to anchors. For example, the party providing the higher anchor (such as a seller) will emphasize the enhancing factors, whereas, the party presenting the lower anchor (such as a buyer) will typically highlight the diminishing factors. A proper evaluation of the enhancing or diminishing factors needs to be performed during the Prepare phase to list down all the factors affecting the price.

When I was selling my four-year-old car, I knew I could put forward a high anchor price. My car had enhancing factors, including an extended warranty that I could pass on to the next buyer, low miles and a great condition for a used car. However, as luck would have it, a couple of diminishing factors negated my high anchor. Just a couple of months ago, the cars for the new year had started selling, and the company introduced a revamped model of my car. I had to settle for a lower price after all.

Market impact on anchors

In some markets, anchors have no impact on the final price due to the bidding process adopted by the market. For instance, in a strong real estate market multiple offers can drive the final price and thus the original anchor price is rendered irrelevant. In these markets, even a low listing price from the seller might generate a higher first offer and consequently a high final sale price.

• • •

Summary

A significant phase of the negotiation is the Engage phase. It is the "make or break" phase, as it is dependent on the successful engagement with the other party or parties in the negotiation. In this chapter, we discussed what are the key considerations for interactions with the other party or parties. We also discussed the importance of framing and the significance of the application of anchors. Another critical part of the engagement phase is the behavior of the parties that we will discuss in Chapter 6. The checklist in Appendix B lists the key steps to be taken during the Engage phase.

CHAPTER 5
Close

After all the hard work in the Prepare and Engage phase, it is crucial that the negotiation is appropriately finalized and closed. In this chapter, we will look at three primary steps to achieve the closure of the negotiation.

The successful closure of the negotiation is dependent on the completion of the three steps below. Let's review these three steps.

Consensus → Record → Handshake

Consensus

In some negotiations, multiple issues and solutions are brought to the table. Parties agree on the bundle of solutions that will be built in the final agreement. This is called the "Consensus" step of the closure process. At the onset, smart negotiators plan the full process to the end. In this process, they understand all the necessary approvals or sign-offs required to move the negotiation to completion. This is valuable where you might have concluded negotiations with a party who would be overruled by others on their side. Often, there are internal sign-offs, for example, a board approval that hampers or delays the process. Being aware of these sign-offs helps to keep track of the success of the negotiation.

It is important to know up front who the decision-maker is and what parties need to provide their consent. In some cases this might even be used as a hardball tactic by some people to get an advantage. As an example, they go through the whole process and then introduce a last-minute condition for a specific approval or sign-off that throws off the negotiating party.

After the U.S. and North Korea talks in Pyongyang in July 2018, Mike Pompeo announced that the negotiations were positive and progress had been made. North Korea, however, did not echo the U.S. reactions. In fact, North Korea went the other way and expressed concerns over the attitude of the U.S. delegations and factors creating distrust. We would never know the full details of the talks, but it was clearly a case where consensus was not achieved at the end of the discussions (Veronica Stracqualursi, CNN, July 7, 2018).

Record

Once all the agreement or consensus is obtained on all the terms and solutions, the next step is to ensure necessary documentation of all agreed terms via a written or electronic document. This ensures that there is no misunderstanding or disagreement after the negotiation is completed. Often in our professional world, discussions are completed at a meeting, but when people walk out of the room, they might have two different versions of what was discussed or that some aspects of the conclusions still might not be clear. It is therefore important to list all the matters that were agreed upon.

Here's a point to consider: How are teams trained to work with multiple contract clauses? The answer is that the teams could create a negotiation playbook explaining all the terms and the acceptable results of those terms. This will help all team members, experienced or new, to address those clauses. A vital point about negotiating these items at the time of recording is not to get stuck with or negotiate each point of discussions. It is better to list all the points and negotiate them as a package.

It is useful to document agreements and solutions at a detailed level. If this is not done, there might be situations where there is lack of clarity, misinterpretation or disagreement. Once a contract is entered into, it is a difficult position for any party that realizes that some terms and conditions are not complete or clear. A case of negotiation with a contractor that my friend narrated highlights this very well. My friend negotiated a contract to lay pavers in his backyard. The full value of the contract was $6,000. The contract was agreed upon and signed. After the start of work and some further deliberation, they now wanted to add a border of pavers of a different color. This did not need any additional effort for the contractor, but he said the amount would now be $7,200. My friend did not have any option but to agree with the increase, but they managed to reduce the cost to $7,000. The question is what did they not do right in this case? What could they do differently? The answer is that they needed to ensure that the contract had clauses and terms for how changes would be handled or for any uncertainties that arise. This would have ensured that the increase could have been negotiated up front and not after the contract was signed.

Another aspect to document is all that was learned from the negotiation.

Handshake

The commitments and agreements that are documented will need to be signed and the final handshake closes the negotiation. The deal takes effect when the final signing occurs. Not all negotiations have a contract, so the close could also be effective via an email.

For a day-to-day negotiation where a contract or email is not required, the handshake happens by reiterating the decision and getting an ok from both sides. The handshake is an assurance that there are no differences in understanding. I once noticed a paper stuck on the side of a cabinet at my friend's home. Upon looking at it a bit closer, I noted that it was the agreement from his negotiation with his son. Additionally, it is important to note that in many cases a final and formal announcement is required after the handshake when, for example, a communication of a large deal needs to be made to shareholders via a press release or to authorities or regulatory bodies. All these vital communication aspects need to be listed as a part of the preparation or determined during the engagement process to ensure that closure is completed.

Finally, the value of an agreement or contractual obligations varies across different cultures. In some cultures the contracts are the primary source of everything agreed upon and can be legally enforced if not adequately implemented. In other cultures even official emails or properly executed agreements might not carry much weight as people take advantage of their positions or connections, and legal enforcement is weak. In one example, a friend in India agreed with the ambassador of the embassy of a foreign country on organizing an event for the embassy. The ambassador confirmed all the details via an official email. This was considered as sufficient confirmation and closure of the negotiation. However, after providing some initial deliverables, the ambassador came back to say that the price would have to be reduced. The ambassador did not think the email confirmation was a final agreement. In most cases embassies are exempt from any enforceable action, and so the ambassador took advantage of her position. At this point, my friend had no strong alternatives. She could either let her efforts go to waste and risk losing her reputation by not continuing on the engagement or she could go ahead to complete the engagement at a lower agreed price trusting that the success of the event would add to her reputation. She finally agreed on the lower price and had a successful event but learned some big lessons along the way.

At this stage, the negotiation discussion might have ended, but in an ideal situation the negotiation is never complete. Continuity of discussions, monitoring and tracking and building relationships always continues. So while we call this the Close phase, it is only meant to close the round of negotiation discussions.

• • •

Summary

As noted at the beginning of this chapter, the negotiation is not complete until it is properly closed. Careful assessment of all the requirements of a proper closure during the Prepare and Engage phase will finally be executed in this phase. I once heard the phrase, "Nothing is agreed until everything is agreed!" at a Harvard negotiation seminar that has stuck with me. After all, if you have put all the effort to come to this stage, you want to realize the benefits of the efforts. The Checklist in Appendix B lists the key steps to consider during the Close phase.

CHAPTER 6
Behaviors

In the previous chapters, we looked at the three phases that form the crux of the negotiation process. In this chapter, I introduce key behaviors that play a highly important role in negotiations. While these are standard behaviors with which we are all familiar, it is critical to look more closely at how these behaviors need to be incorporated all through the process of negotiation. Negotiating is about bringing the right attitude to the table. The behaviors are vital, having the potential to make or break a negotiation. These behaviors apply throughout the three phases of negotiation and must be considered along the process. Whether in a distributive or integrative negotiation (approaches to negotiation as explained in Chapter 3), the appropriate behaviors are necessary.

A key element of behaviors is gaining trust of the other party. Therefore we will start with a discussion of trust. We will then review how verbal and non-verbal communication assists in the success of negotiations. In the latter part of this chapter, we will discuss culture and styles that are also essential components of behaviors demonstrated during negotiations.

Trust

In any sphere of life, it is paramount to build trust and credibility, and negotiations are no different. Do you think any negotiation will move forward or be acceptable to either party if there is no trust? Let's assume you are in a market where there are hundreds of sellers, each selling similar or same items. From which seller are you more likely to buy their product? Isn't the seller who you trust more likely to be your preferred seller?

We expect from others actions that instill trust. It is logical, therefore, that when we are at the negotiation table, specific attention needs to be placed on our appropriate behaviors that generate trust of the other party. Bear in mind that it is trust that helps us build long-term relationships and ensures success over a long period of time. Remember, however, that trust takes a long time to build, but it could be broken very quickly.

Some such actions that will cultivate trust are explained below.

- Understand the other: Trust comes from being respected, and respect comes from not only being proficient at what you do, but also demonstrating that you understand the other party and would like to partner with them. The feel-good factor that is essential in finalizing a deal results from being considerate to the other party's feelings and making things work. This contributes positively to building trust.

- Develop relationships first when dealing with certain cultures: In many cultures, the negotiations do not even start in the first few meetings. Relationship-building and earning credibility are primary objectives. As an example, Guanxi in the Chinese environment (we discuss Guanxi in more detail in Chapter 7) relates to the development of relationships and can only be sustained over long periods of time by maintaining the trust and credibility between the parties. A friend described his approach in negotiating with stakeholders in eastern and southeast Asia where the first few meetings do not even touch on the actual agenda. As his job involved requesting sponsorship from stakeholders, building relationships was primary before he talked business.

- Focus on ethics: Trust can be earned by demonstrating integrity and fairness. Fairness results from thoughtful consideration to the needs of all parties. As G. Richard Shell remarked in *Bargaining for Advantage* (2nd edition, page 63), "Generosity begets generosity, fairness begets fairness, and unfairness ought to beget a firm response." Fairness is an important component in the process of negotiation and paying specific attention to what all parties need and building solutions accordingly will help in developing trust.

- Be flexible: Flexibility provides the objectivity and reliability that is necessary in long-term relationships. Flexibility is required throughout the negotiation process, and its absence can hamper relationships and derail a negotiation.

In a story of an established company (let's call it Company A) and its negotiation with a high-profile client, the value of flexibility and compromise is accentuated. Company A is a technology service provider and a market leader in its industry. The client was working on developing a new product and wanted to partner with Company A. They had expressed their interests of having a simple design of the product, but Company A insisted on keeping the complicated details on the product. Over eighteen months were spent on the deal, but in the end the client found it hard to work with Company A and opted to partner with a competitor who was willing to accommodate the client's requests. Company A's president later admitted that they had been inflexible by sticking to their bureaucratic process.

- Be open to compromise: In many cases, when the parties are very close to finalizing the negotiation, compromise might help to take it past the finish line. The key is to not give up at that stage for an egoistic position. Be open to compromise when the situation demands so that efforts, time, and cost to reach that stage are not wasted. However, compromise should not be a substitute or excuse for a serious effort in negotiations. A question that is commonly asked is "If I end up compromising, how do I make sure I do not regret it?" This is a great question and in this instance make sure that the compromise does not adversely impact your objectives or results in an unfavorable outcome.

- Show presence: Trust and credibility can also be developed by showing commitment to make a deal happen for the benefit of all parties. Such commitment is best demonstrated by showing presence. In this day of remote negotiations across the globe, the effectiveness of showing presence is constantly debated. Presence (or face-to-face negotiations) is a powerful component of negotiations and is always more effective than remote negotiation. To the extent possible, it is advisable to negotiate in person. The power of presence was highlighted in the Google-AOL example in Chapter 3.

Trust aids with the success of any negotiation. How does trust help with this?

- Earn respect: As stated above, gaining the trust of the other party helps you earn respect, which in turn helps in a smooth conduct of the negotiation discussions.
- Build association: Gaining trust also helps in building a long-term association, thereby ensuring that future interactions are effective.
- Create positive vibes: A strong trust builds positive mood and creates the vibes needed to ensure that the discussions run smoothly and generate productive results.
- Avoid biases: Two-way trust helps to avoid any biases that either party might possess.

What happens if you do not have trust?

In a negotiation, trust is assumed. However, if there are indications that either party cannot be adequately trusted, then some measures have to be introduced that will reinforce the loss of trust. Such measures are listed here below:

- Document everything: Record all interactions, keep minutes, document terms and conditions via email or contract or otherwise.
- Request external assurance: Request assurance from a third party such as a reference, guarantor, etc.
- Consequences: Often there are some consequences that can be added to ensure that the other party delivers on their promises. Such consequences could be favorable (commonly known as "carrot") or adverse (commonly known as "stick").
- Monitor regularly: All agreements should be monitored for adequate performance. Another form

of monitoring is post-transaction warranty, a commonly applicable trust-generating measure.

Communication

Communication is another criterion that plays a salient role in all our interactions and is of utmost significance in all negotiations. Without proper communication there is no chance of negotiation. The key to effective communication is to find the right communication lines. In many cultures it is only the person of power with whom to communicate, and therefore is something that should be considered upfront during preparation. However, in other cases it might be possible to build communication lines with other team members.

The best time to build effective communication channels is right at the start of engaging with the party. Often, icebreakers and similar exercises can be introduced to open the door to better communication. Furthermore, communication lines can be created through references or mediators if it becomes difficult to communicate with the other party directly. Personal styles also play a role in their communication. As we look at the styles later in this chapter, we will see that a person with the Avoiding style blocks off communication and thereby renders the negotiation ineffective.

Verbal

We will now look at some of the verbal communication essentials that will help drive forward the negotiations. Several of these elements need attention to ensure you communicate properly.

- First of all, proper communication starts with the ability to be a good listener. Listening is one of the most effective abilities that one can easily adopt for maximum benefits if executed genuinely. I heard a relevant comment: "Listening is not waiting for your turn to speak."

- It is a primary requirement for smooth communication. I asked a mentor how she was able to keep matters calm even when the discussions were contentious. She replied that she listens intently while giving the other party the utmost chance to speak. Have you ever been in a situation when you have spoken on a tough topic and then realized you missed some points? My mentor shared this feeling with me, saying that she asked the other party in follow-up meetings if they had any more points to highlight. Quite often they come back with a few more points that she listens to carefully, thus ensuring that the other party has gotten the full opportunity to speak.

- Listening has two clear benefits: 1) the other party feels better that you were considerate to ask, and 2) they would be able to express their views freely, making them open-minded. Furthermore, listening produces more insights into their needs and thereby allows you to effectively modify your points in the negotiation. It helps to gain respect from people and build relationships.

- In order to get the most information out of the engagement with the other party, the best approach is to ask open-ended questions (i.e., questions that cannot be answered in one or two words) that prompt the other party to provide a response. This is a good way to draw out detailed responses to questions that help to derive solutions for a successful negotiation. Curiosity is useful in any negotiation, and asking questions skillfully helps to support curiosity with relevant information. As an example, compare two ways of asking the same question but yielding different responses: A manager once asked, "Did we address the delays in responding to the client's queries?" That question could have been asked more skillfully to yield useful information thus "How did we address the delays in responding to the client's queries?"

- In addition to clearly communicating the merits of your negotiation discussion, a crucial part of communication is to highlight the benefits that the other party will derive from the negotiation. In common professional terms, it is known as WIIFM (What's In It For Me). Clearly articulating the benefits is important to gain the trust of the other party. This implies the importance of the choice of words.

- Ask for clarification and elaboration, and request relevant examples. Repeat and rephrase what the other party had said to confirm correct understanding. This is to ensure you have taken into account the interests of the other party and to avoid any differences in understanding.

- As well, studies show that humor is a powerful element in communicating and connecting with people. It adds an angle to communication that facilitates smoother conversations.

- When it comes to communication with people across cultures and languages, the nuances of cross-border communication need to be followed. There are specific considerations to keep in mind. In order to overcome language barriers, interpreters should be utilized to assure complete clarity of discussions.

Non-verbal (actions, emotions and body language)

Another vital element of communication is non-verbal behavior such as emotions and body language. Intelligence Quotient (IQ) and Emotional Intelligence or Quotient (EQ) are well-known, and each has its own merit when it comes to engagement with others. Often, people consider IQ to have the upper hand, while I consider EQ to be essential as a complement to the IQ. Emotional Intelligence (EQ) is a crucial aspect of all interactions. Both IQ and EQ are not adequate by themselves.

- Focus on body language: Your body language is vital in conversations. Many cues come from observing others' body language. Your own approach can be adjusted according to the body language demonstrated by the other party.
- Control over emotions: Effectively managing one's own emotions is paramount. At the same time, while it is necessary to be considerate to the other party's feelings, subtly calling out highly-charged emotions of the other party helps to restrain the emotions and discussions to a smooth conclusion. Along this line of thought, it is key to avoid hostility, as it can break any communications.
- Confidence: Another primary behavior is to beam with confidence. The confidence ensuing from body language drives a point home. Confidence also leads to composure, so it is important that one feels confident going into the discussion. It is, however, critical to understand the fine line between being confident and appearing overconfident.

In addition to these demeanors, there are a couple of key considerations in the behavior required in negotiations—culture and styles of the parties. We will look at the influence of culture next in this chapter. The Cultural considerations are complemented by an understanding of one's own style as well as the style of the other party. We will discuss style in the latter part of this chapter.

• • •

Culture

What is culture?

Culture represents the values or behavior of a group of people that become the norm, due to constant socialization and repetitive application.

Negotiating across different cultures is an important skill in today's globalized environment. The fast pace of business interaction growth across markets in all parts of the world calls for emphasis on the cultural aspects in the negotiation process.

What is **Culture Inclination** (CI)?

It is the ability to relate to and work effectively in culturally diverse situations. It can be developed by paying close attention to the norms of the other person's culture.

I discussed IQ and EQ while discussing emotions in the previous section. However, I believe that Culture Inclination ("CI") supports both the EQ and IQ in every aspect of life these days. We interact with people of different cultures, and it matters heavily if we understand, be sensitive to, and adopt to an extent, the cultural aspects that apply to the other party.

The impact of culture on negotiations is a vast topic and a thorough understanding would require a full book by itself. In this chapter, we look at the significance of culture in global negotiations at a higher level. As you read on, you will notice that culture is complicated, since different types of cultures could influence the other party.

Dealing with people from different cultures needs careful thought and understanding of their cultures. Behaviors are significantly different when you are dealing with different cultures. In any negotiation across cultures, a vital prerequisite is to read, understand, and be specifically mindful of these behaviors. Some such behaviors are described below.

- Impressions: The style of meeting and greeting a person varies widely across various cultures. The adage "First impressions are the most lasting impressions" signifies how crucial it is to evaluate the approach to meeting and greeting. Presentation will play a big role in how your negotiation discussions will progress. After the first meeting, the approach may be re-evaluated to meet the benchmark set by the other party. A big part of this factor is the "dressing etiquette." I was informed by a participant at my workshops how her father appeared as a strong personality in negotiations due to how he presented himself and how he dressed up on most occasions. In many cultures, being dressed up provides a significant boost in the image that drives different behaviors.
- Body contact and body language: Along the same lines as impressions are the touch, contact and body language. Thoughtful preparation and study of cultures can prevent behaviors that harm reputation. Sign language also needs proper attention.
- Punctuality: Focus on time considerations differ by culture. It is important to know the cultural requirements in terms of focus on time. In some cultures, rigorous adherence to time is a prerequisite, while in other cultures there is no emphasis on time sensitivity.

- Other considerations: There are several criteria that impact cultural behaviors, including gift giving, level of assertiveness or being pushy and group vs. individualism. Specific awareness of these criteria based on the other party's culture is beneficial to the overall success of the negotiations.

As we can see from above, several considerations come into the picture when dealing across different cultures. For the cross-cultural negotiation process, all through the Prepare, Engage, and Close phases of your negotiation, identify and attend to differences in cultural dimensions. If not adequately addressed and/or managed, these differences can give rise to adverse behaviors, generate negative results such as loss of trust, and lead to a breakdown of negotiations.

An interesting story is narrated in *Too Big to Fail,* by Andrew Ross Sorkin, about the negotiation between Lehman Brothers and Korea Development Bank (KDB), a state-owned bank in South Korea. A short excerpt of the story is shared below, but I would highly recommend reading the full story in the book. A movie adaptation of this story was also released in 2011.

In June 2008, Lehman Brothers was in trouble. The stock had fallen 22.6 percent since May 2008. Raising capital was desperately required. Lehman was in talks with KDB for investment. For KDB, acquiring assets of Lehman was an important step to becoming a global player. Min Euoo Sung, the head of KDB, had a grand vision of a global name for KDB. The leader culture at KDB played heavily in this decision. Lehman had a series of discussions with KDB starting in June and concluding in August. In the first week of August, Min and his team arrived in Manhattan for an all-important meeting between KDB and Lehman officials. Herbert "Bart" McDade, President and COO of Lehman, led the discussions with KDB. Richard "Dick" Fuld, the CEO, was requested to be the "missing man" who could come in at the end to "top off the deal." Min and KDB were a bit apprehensive of the real estate portfolio of Lehman, but Lehman was desperate to get the deal closed at the earliest. The parties inched closer to getting a deal done.

At that stage, in a discussion with Dick Fuld, Bart McDade remarked that Min was not sure of the real estate portfolio. On hearing this, Dick could not hold himself back and stormed into the meeting room right at the time the letter of intent was being discussed and started talking about the real estate portfolio. He used phrases such as "you are making a big mistake" and "you must have looked at them in the wrong way." Koreans found his approach obtrusive. A deal that was being nurtured with the South Koreans over two days fell apart due to a display of assertiveness (refer to Assertiveness dimension in the GLOBE study below). Credibility had become an issue. Min was not happy about the way they were treated and how the meeting was conducted. It came to no one's surprise that the Koreans abandoned the deal and walked away.

It is pertinent to discuss the effectiveness of influencing techniques that we studied in the previous chapter across different cultures. In my workshops I have heard that some of the influencing techniques might not work in some of the Asian countries. The power of reciprocation, for instance, is not that strong in some cultures, and as a result, the technique might not be as effective in some negotiations across cultures. Similarly, the "Promise" technique (discussed in Chapter 7) might also be a bit blunt in some cultures where the value of promise might not be binding.

Culture can be imbibed from different sources:
- Country culture, namely, the culture of one's home nation. It has substantial influence on the general behavior due to the assimilation of cultural norms from a young age. When a person moves to another

nation, the influence of the nation the person moves to starts to grow over a period of time.

- Society culture, namely, the culture of the society's practices and beliefs. Clear rules and norms apply to societies or communities that might be more nuanced than the country culture. The society culture has a heavier influence than the country culture.
- Organizational culture, that is, practices and beliefs which affect people who are part of an organization such as a school, a corporate organization or a religious body having a strong culture and capacity to influence the members.
- Leader culture, that is, any organization, either formal or informal, that has a strong leader inculcates values and behaviors in all the members.

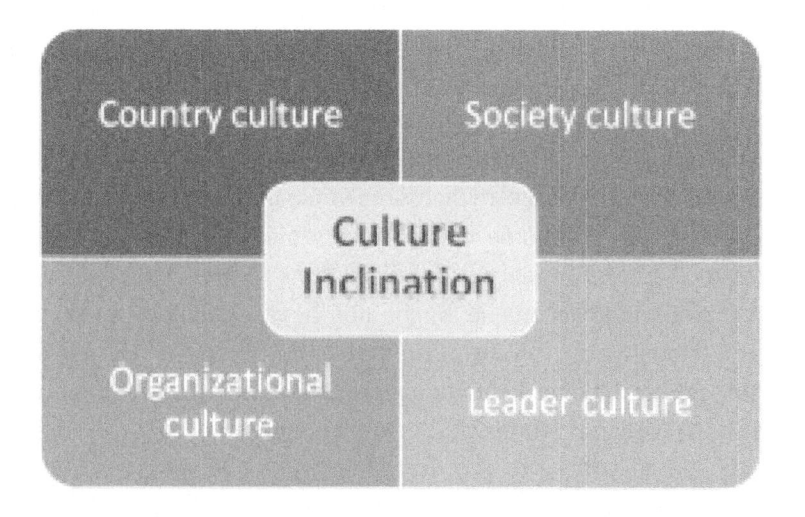

Country culture	Society culture
Organizational culture	Leader culture

Culture Inclination

Country Culture

Let's now take a closer look at country/national cultures. The impact of a person's country culture is significant due to the values and behaviors instilled from a young age. It is one of the primary sources of values and behaviors. We will discuss this in a bit more detail using the analysis of the GLOBE study that I believe has generated riveting results around national cultures. This study was compiled by R. J. House, P. J. Hanges, M. Javidan, P. W. Dorfman, and V. Gupta, and was completed in 2004. Based on a review of the study, we will become aware that the findings of the study are still applicable even to this day.

Of course, times are changing, and some of the results of the GLOBE study might start to be outdated. National culture's influence has been diluted through globalization, international education and travel, the Internet, and ongoing professional relationships around the world. What's more, it is important to note that some countries might have more than one culture. The study attempts to take that into consideration by breaking some countries into two different parts. In my opinion it is important to be aware of the country culture's aspects and consider them as one additional source of information during the Prepare and Engage phases, while not completely relying on the generalization of country culture as the primary driver of the negotiation process.

The study was conducted across nine dimensions covering sixty-two countries. The countries were categorized in bands from A to D for each dimension. The higher the indication or applicability of the dimensions for each country results in the higher score assigned to that country. The highest scores are in Band A and so on. Refer to the GLOBE study for a comprehensive look at the nine dimensions and country rankings for those dimensions.

A review of the dimensions below provides an understanding of the nine dimensions and their applicability. As we look at these dimensions, I spell out the impact that these dimensions could have on our negotiations and how we can address the effect of the national culture.

Power Distance

This dimension represents distance created by power accumulation at higher levels vs. the lower levels. The higher the score the higher the distance of power across the levels and vice versa.

In a negotiation, the actions to address the power distance in countries with higher scores are as follows:
- Know who calls the shots.
- Send high-power or higher status persons for negotiations with high-power distance.
- Assess and cater to the interests of the highest authority person.
- Communicate with the high-power person when dealing with high-power distance.

Uncertainty Avoidance

This dimension provides the measure by which a culture or society tends to view the unpredictability of future events. The higher the score, the higher the tendency to stick to a standard approach and avoid uncertainty and vice versa.

Actions to address situations where there is high uncertainty avoidance are as follows:
- Include assurances for unpredictability in high uncertainty avoidance cultures.
- Follow a structured approach for negotiation in high uncertainty avoidance cultures— agendas, meeting minutes, proper documentation, and anything else that will help clear up uncertainty.

Humane Orientation

This dimension demonstrates the value assigned in a culture to being fair, altruistic, generous, caring and kind to others. The higher the score, the higher the attention towards humane behavior and vice versa.

Considerations of impacting humane orientation on negotiations is as follows:
- Pay attention to the degree of fairness for people.
- Consider devising solutions to benefit people in a high humane orientation culture.
- Focus on the issues in a low humane orientation culture.

Assertiveness
This dimension depicts the level of assertiveness of the culture as well as the resulting confrontation and aggressiveness in their interactions with others. The higher the score, the higher the culture of assertiveness and vice versa.

Assertiveness can be addressed in the following actions:
- Understand that assertiveness is a norm in high assertiveness cultures.
- Consider direct and to-the-point behaviors in high assertiveness cultures.
- Respectfully address assertiveness or confrontation when dealing with high assertiveness cultures.

Collectivism (Institutional, Societal)
This dimension represents encouragement and reward for focus on collective action at institutional or societal level. The higher the score, the higher the level of organizational/societal collectivism and vice versa.

Actions to impact negotiations are as follows:
- Focus on goals at organization or society level, rather than individuals in high collectivism cultures.

- Build solutions that benefit the collective in high-collectivism cultures.

Collectivism (In-group, Family)
This dimension represents the value that the culture assigns to pride, loyalty, and cohesiveness that members have in their groups or families. The higher the score, the higher the focus on in-group/family collectivism and vice versa.

Actions to impact negotiations are as follows:
- Focus on goals at family or group level rather than individuals in high-collectivism cultures.
- Respect the loyalty toward the group or family in high collectivism cultures.
- Build solutions that benefit the collective in high collectivism cultures.
- Additional time is required when working with high collectivism cultures.

Gender egalitarianism
This dimension highlights the degree of acceptance of gender equality. The higher the score, the higher the level of gender equality and vice versa.

Impact on negotiations:
- Respect differences in gender egalitarianism across cultures.
- Focus on devising solutions that cater to gender equality.

Future orientation
This dimension presents the emphasis on future orientation, such as building and investing for the future and forward planning. The higher the score, the higher the forward thinking and vice versa.

Impact on negotiations:
- Building solutions that focus on future-oriented behaviors in high future orientation cultures.
- Longer term perspective and gains are important in high future orientation cultures.
- Reward for longer-term thinking and planning.

Performance orientation

This dimension represents the emphasis and reward for performance improvement and continuous focus on excellence. The higher the score, the higher the focus on performance and vice versa.

Impact on negotiations:
- Expectation is to deliver consistent and quality performance in high performance orientation cultures.
- Interpersonal relations are not the focus in high performance orientation cultures.
- Striving for continuously improved performance.
- Building solutions that reward based on performance when dealing with high performance orientation cultures.

Society culture

Society cultures exist as a subset of country cultures. In many countries, there are numerous societies that have different cultures. Society culture refers to the values and norms in smaller sections of countries, such as a region or a state and in ethnic groups. Society cultures can be significantly different within the same country. For example, in a country such as Singapore diverse society cultures exist among the Chinese, Malay and Indian ethnic groups. Once you know the societal differences in cultures, you can formulate negotiation strategies to cater to those cultural differences.

When one is dealing with people from another country, it is necessary to direct focus on the combination of country culture and society culture of the other party. However, when dealing with the other party within the country, the consideration of society culture can be a valuable guide to understanding behaviors of the other party.

Organizational culture

People are drawn to organizations due to a strong culture, i.e., the values and behaviors. Such organizations could be companies, religious bodies or institutions. Values are the foundation that is established for people in the organization to follow, and behaviors represent the practice of the culture at every level in the organization. A vital piece of behavior is the people's spirit or intent to adhere to the culture. The leadership team and all employees contribute to the establishment of the organizational culture.

The key goal of developing a strong organizational culture is to inculcate the right values in people. Some examples of values that organizations instill are:
1. Drive results through strong execution.
2. Focus on the customer.
3. Encourage innovation and creativity.
4. Make continuous learning a priority.
5. Embrace change.
6. Listen to all employees.
7. Value diversity.
8. Celebrate success.
9. Be ethical and fair.

Note that organizational culture is influenced to a certain extent by the national or society culture.

The impact of organizational cultures is so prominent that any drastic change in the culture can hinder performance, productivity, thinking and motivation. Often, we observe that when a larger and more mature company acquires a smaller company, they prefer to keep the smaller company independent as long as possible so that their organizational culture is intact.

The organizational culture drives the necessary behaviors, whether negotiating within or outside the organization, in order to negotiate effectively. Specifically, within the organization, the values and behaviors can be a crucial guide and reminder to follow in the negotiations. For example, if the organization culture is focused on innovation and creativity, such values should be called upon while negotiating with the internal stakeholders. Conversely, while negotiating outside the organization it is beneficial to study the other party's organizational culture or gauge the culture during the negotiation.

Leader Culture

The last source where people adopt a culture is from a leader. The leader could be the head of the team, CEO of the company, or the leader of the state or country. The leader culture is the vision, values, and actions of the leader that convert into the behavior for the people following the leader.

To an extent, the leader culture is derived from the leader's style. The style converts into values and behaviors that become the culture. We have seen many strong leaders whose values influence the behaviors and practices of their followers and result in the creation of a culture. In certain situations, knowing and understanding the leader's culture helps to determine appropriate negotiation strategies. This is particularly applicable when you are negotiating with the head of a family or negotiating with a team member who belongs to a strong leader's team.

In the next section, we will look at different styles and the impact these styles have on negotiations.

• • •

Styles

Culture can have a heavy impact on understanding the other party and aligning behavior in a negotiation, but so does assessing styles. As pointed out in Chapter 2, individual styles matter in how the parties conduct and behave in the negotiations. This section discusses styles in more detail. The negotiating style varies by individual, and attending to differences in styles therefore becomes a serious consideration. These differences, if not adequately addressed and/or managed during the negotiation discussions, can result in adverse reactions and behaviors.

Firstly, it is important that we know our own style. I highly encourage readers to take a style assessment that is available in *Bargaining for Advantage,* by G. Richard Shell, to understand your style. Secondly, it is imperative to understand the style of the other party. The idea is to be able to know in advance via preparation what the style of the decision-maker on the other side is and to understand our own style. A good understanding of our own dominant style and the style of the other provides the ability to devise strategies and arrive at necessary actions to cater to the style. Styles are generally inherent, but in most cases the style also develops into a hybrid over time with more experience and practice.

There is a saying from the famous, age-old Chinese military treatise, Sun Zi Bing Fa a.k.a. Sun Tzu's *Art of War:* "Zhi bi zhi ji, bai zhan bai sheng." It signifies a very important message that applies to modern-day business and directly to negotiations. It translates to: "Know the other party, know yourself; hundred battles, hundred won." A friend also introduced me to another commonly used phrase "Zhi bi zhi ji, bai fa bai zhong," which translates to "Know the other party, know yourself; every target achieved." In simple terms these phrases basically mean that in order to be successful in negotiations, it is important to know the other party as much as it is to know oneself. Knowing the other party will help evaluate their moves, which is primary in negotiations. As a part of knowing the other party, it is important to know their vision, leader's style, strengths and weaknesses, competitors, partners, etc. This vital knowledge can help drive the strategies in negotiation.

An example from the trade tariffs between the U.S. and China during 2018-2019 comes to mind. The U.S. started by imposing tariffs on China, but it is vital to evaluate the strengths of China. While the U.S. might have thought that this was the right strategy in the negotiation with China, having had a similar success with Mexico, this is where knowing the other party is critical. China is capable of a strong counter, and this is not beneficial to anybody in the long term. The tariff barriers caused a ripple effect across the global business and political environment. After months of stand-offs, there was no conclusion to this tariff war, and it created a big uncertainty in the global economic scenario.

There are five key types of styles commonly cited in style analysis as referenced in books and on the Internet. We will review these styles, and I will present my understanding of how these styles differ and what bearing the different styles have on negotiations.

Collaborating or "It's a win-win" style
This style refers to the inclination to work collaboratively when a matter or issue is brought up in a negotiation. Solutions are derived based on joint partnership and agreement to achieve mutual gains. Specifically, this style calls for:
- Focusing on both parties' interests; and/or
- Nurturing a long-term partnership; and/or
- Building trust by "growing the pie."

Most commonly, people with this style frequently ask questions to understand the other party's interest in providing mutually acceptable options. How do you identify people with the Collaborating style? Some specific criteria and characteristics include:
- They say, "Let's work together to identify the underlying issues and solutions."
- They openly display a collective effort to address all concerns.
- They make a concerted effort to achieve the interests of both or all.

If you identify the other person to have this style, it is worthwhile to adopt a similar style to get the best results from the negotiation. While dealing with a person of this style, specific attention should be paid to mutual benefits, and these should be built in the negotiation discussions. Take the cues for partnering and arrive at common solutions. Another important aspect of this style is that it results in creativity. The collaboration and focus on "win-win" brings the best out of these individuals. Other styles should also learn to adopt this collaborative approach to the extent possible.

Let's now look at an example. A multiparty negotiation involves a leader and four team members who are contributing to the prioritization of a list of system issues during the development of a new system. The leader plays an intelligent move. Instead of driving the decision on each issue and for her to make a final call, she asks the four persons to brainstorm on each issue. She builds the collaboration mindset, taking the interests of all parties into consideration.

In the case of conflicts, this style expects spending time to discuss options. Problem-solving is the main criterion in a conflict situation with this style. It takes time to resolve conflicts, as many options are discussed on the table. The focus is to be able to come up with solutions for mutual benefits. Unfortunately, there are many cases where this style might have to adopt a competitive style or other styles. This is unavoidable and might also need some practice.

Compromising or "give-and-take" style
This style refers to behavior that the other party's needs should be accepted when they seem more reasonable in some situations, but expect to get your points answered in other situations. The idea is to give something important to the other party but call for an exchange. In many cases the expected result is to reach a middle point so that both parties walk away feeling that they got a bargain. Many people think of this style as the "win-win" because it results in getting a deal that both parties accept. However, this style may not create the mutually beneficial solutions that are generated by the collaborating style.

In this style:
- Objective is to share with others while getting back some; and/or
- Willing to give some in exchange; and/or
- Believe in reciprocation.

As with most compromises, both parties might not always walk away knowing that they got the best deal. In some cases, when they are done with the deal, their gut feeling is that it could have been better. But they know that under the circumstances they got some and gave some.

Some ways to identify a person with this style are:
- They say, "Let's work on a compromise that helps us both."
- They give some but expect or ask for some.
- They are interested in getting to the middle ground.

While working with a person who demonstrates this style, keep in mind what you can provide that is valuable to him/her/them, but at the same time try to achieve what you want. Support their interests and needs in the negotiation to the extent possible, and they will do the same for you.

In general, most kids are the best proponents of the compromise style. How often do we have a scenario where the negotiation between a kid and a parent or between kids ends up in a compromise? A recent example from a friend illustrates this. The kid was extraordinary in mathematics. The parents recognized this and sent the kid for two math enrichment classes. The kid performed well, but in discussion with his friends he said, "I am not interested in mathematics, and I attend only because my parents insist." In the fear of not burning out the kid too quickly, the father came up with an idea. He said to his son, "All the math that you do is good, but we need to make sure you do something you enjoy. Would you like to do something that you enjoy?" The son said "Yeah! I would really like to go to basketball classes." After a bit of thought and planning, the father agreed to undertake the cost and effort for the son's request for basketball classes but on the condition that the son continued with the math classes and received a certain score. Here we have a healthy compromise that demonstrates the style that works with kids. In this case the father also adapted well to the compromising style.

Another parent once remarked that the easiest and most effective way to negotiate with kids is to "bribe" them. He said, "Every parent has adopted this as a method of influencing when a situation demands a quick resolution." While I absolutely understood what he was referring to, I was compelled to correct it and frame it more accurately. When you propose to a kid something in return for a request or an action, it is a negotiator's way of providing options and solutions to the kid. It is also bringing out the underlying compromising style of the kids into action, ensuring that the outcome meets the mutual needs of both parties. The offer to the child should not become a kind of promise that the parent will be forced to provide in all similar, future circumstances. The parents need to carefully decide what they want to offer to the child based on the situation and to provide a caveat in advance that it is only meant for that case. Mixing up the options will avoid being stuck to providing the same item or benefit in all cases, regardless of the situation.

In the case of conflicts, this style expects exchanging and sharing concessions. The idea is not to get the best, but to reach a meaningful middle ground. As discussed under Collaborating, this style might also need to adopt a different style in some cases. Furthermore, if the counterpart uses a hardball tactic to take a higher stake, a compromising style might take the hit, so it is useful to be prepared for this situation.

Competing or "It's my way or the highway" style
This style is typically the aggressive style where the primary criterion is to prove a point and achieve their own points. For people in this style, the perspectives are:

- Focus on their own interests; and/or
- Be assertive right from the beginning; and/or
- Be open to using hardball tactics to accomplish objectives.

Negotiation with this style could prove challenging. Dominance and aggression are demonstrated right from the start, and careful consideration should be made if you want to match the behavior. Intimidation is another tactic that a person of this style often uses. Emotions can run high in these situations. In many cases, if two people with this style engage in a negotiation, there is a high likelihood of a stalemate.

While sometimes being competitive is important, in most cases the competing style could possibly derail the negotiation if the other party loses trust. A competing style person should try to adopt a collaborating or even a compromising style in certain circumstances to be an effective negotiator.

A person with a competing style displays some of the following characteristics or expresses their opinion as below:
- They strive to achieve what they want and stick to it; and/or
- Always ask for more or for concessions without talking about giving any; and/or
- They might say, "I believe this is how we should do it" or "I believe I can provide the best value in this case" or "I think the best result of this negotiation is if I can get this."

When dealing with a person of this style, it is important to determine the strategy. The options you have are to also play tough. However, if it's not your regular style to play tough, this could backfire. In this case you have to be upfront and control the situation by being calm. Do not get intimidated or forced to make hasty decisions. Share rules at the beginning or as you go along suggesting we would collaborate to arrive at solutions. If required, call out the behavior and take a break to regroup later.

In the case of conflicts, a party practicing this style expects getting the upper hand. While this might not sound like a good way for a negotiation discussion to go, there are ways to persist with a person of this style. Multiple options can be derived and offered. Often, some options that might be important to a competing person might not be difficult to provide. A good analysis of these options and providing them as you go will help a person of this style to calm down and start being more open to the discussion. This, however, might be easier said than done. In those conflict situations where the likelihood of an agreement with this style is not looking feasible, the resulting alternatives are mediation or legal suits. In the age of kings and empires, competing styles would often result in wars. In the modern business context, war is replaced by lawsuits.

Accommodating or "Will do it for you" style
This style refers to the scenario where there is a likelihood of being heavily influenced by what the other party needs and as such runs the risk of giving in to their requests. The primary goal of these individuals is to grow and/or maintain relationships. Some of the factors that play a role in this style are:
- Generally have higher EQ, which focuses on relationships;
- Impacted by feelings such as trust and empathy; and/or
- May sometimes even make decisions that leave value on the table to maintain relationships.

People with an accommodating style generally arrive at a discussion with the goal of managing relationships. The accomplishment is in making it through the negotiation without jeopardizing feelings and relationships. In the process they might defer gratification or lose some leverage, but that is secondary in their minds. Concessions are frequently made by people with this style. I have heard cases and have observed some people who have announced concessions before the other party has stated their position. People of this style are most likely to be taken advantage of by other styles.

Some typical characteristics or ways to identify a person of this style are:
- They tend to agree more with the other party; and/or
- They also give more concessions; and/or

- They say, "Sure. You are right. I understand where you are coming from."

While dealing with a person of accommodating style, you will need to clearly understand their interests through a process of asking questions and active listening. It is useful to make sure that they understand all aspects and that they are given a chance to express their opinion.

I will open a page from my personal experience as an example of the Accommodating style. A few years ago, long before I focused on the science and art of negotiation, I got a job offer in another country. The salary package in the new job was equivalent to the old job, but since it involved relocation and related benefits, along with a lower tax rate in the other location, I had already committed in my mind that the salary was good. In my mind I came up with different reasons to deem that the new salary was adequate and I didn't want to affect relationships with the new manager and HR. This is the essence of the accommodating style.

Looking back, I tried to answer some of the basic questions
- Did I leave value on the table? Yes, I did.
- Would I do anything differently if I was in that position now? The answer is yes. Based on the knowledge of negotiation practices, techniques, and behaviors, I would certainly negotiate differently now.

In the case of conflicts with people of this style, it is beneficial to discuss relationships and build on the emotional quotient. Attention to emotions will address the way forward in negotiations.

Avoiding or "I lose, but you also lose" style
Finally, this style refers to the tendency to avoid any direct conversations that have any element of unpredictability or challenges. Primary aspects of this style are below:

- Direct "to-the-point" interaction; and/or
- Avoid confrontation or leave it to others; and/or
- Procrastinate and delay tough decisions.

People with this style tend to leave difficult conversations aside or defer those conversations to others. They prefer to quickly get to a decision. There is no focus on enlarging the array of options. In many cases people with this style would just walk away after discussing the positions of each side and abruptly end the negotiation.

Some ways that a person of this style would behave or express their opinion are:
- They shut down in difficult conversations or conflict situations, becoming quiet; and/or
- They refuse or decline attempts to move forward or meet; and/or
- They are more likely to ask for a timeout or say, "Let's discuss this next week" or "I would need my manager in the discussion to move further on this."

When engaging with persons of this style, it is important to persist with them. Initiating discussions with positive aspects for them that drive towards building options and asking leading questions might help with getting a response. Give them enough time to make decisions. Showing that you care and are there to support them will give them comfort.

In the case of conflicts, it is beneficial to give the persons of this style some time and engage them subsequently. If this does not seem to work, then finding other routes or escalating would be the only other options.

Kids are generally proponents of this style. After working with them to address points that might be holding them back, they might switch to the Compromising style.

My daughter primarily demonstrates the Avoiding style. It is difficult in negotiations since getting a response sometimes becomes extremely difficult. In these situations, there are different options available in a negotiation, and it is good to wait for the right opportunity to steer the negotiation in the right direction.

My daughter was on the girls' cricket team in her previous school, and her keen interest in the sport grew. A few months ago, after having taken a break from cricket, she started cricket coaching again. Recently, the school team manager at her middle school asked me if she would be interested in joining the school team. There was an inter-school cricket tournament in which any school could register if they had 12 players on a team. While it was beneficial to the team, as they needed adequate players, it was a lucky break for my daughter as she had just started training a few months earlier. I immediately understood the value of this opportunity for her and agreed to register her for the team.

Now commenced the negotiation with my daughter to play on the school cricket team. As mentioned, she had a keen interest in the sport. Nevertheless, she was apprehensive. She had practiced with the school team that was comprised mostly of boys, and they played hard. She was not comfortable practicing with them. When I discussed with her about registering for the school team, she was adamant that she would not play with the team. I told her that I had committed to paying the registration fees and will go ahead, but she could choose not to play. She was indifferent and stood firm with her position. It was a difficult negotiation.

A few days passed, and I had registered her without her confirmation. I had already paid the registration fees, so I had no other alternative. I knew that persistence works well in these situations. I had to use a different way to frame the discussion. My objective was to get her to go on the field.

A couple of days before the first match, I got a much-needed opportunity while dealing with the Avoiding style. It was a lucky break in a seemingly lost cause. I read a message that the committee was looking for parent volunteers to help in the matches. This was my chance to try a different approach. I told her that I had volunteered to be the umpire (referee) in the match, and she could come just to watch the match. She agreed.

Step 1 achieved in the negotiation to bring her to the field. At the game she watched me on the field as the umpire and watched her team play the game. She realized that it was fun to play. At the end of the match, I told her that she just needed to be on the field to get comfortable. I eased her concerns by telling her that she would not need to bat or bowl, as her team was strong. So, she agreed to go and field. Step 2 was accomplished, as she was on the field for the next game. It was now just a matter of time before she got more confidence, and then she would also agree to go out and bat or bowl. Building confidence by helping her gain comfort was critical. The negotiation to bring her to the field was successful by understanding her interests and attending to her preferences. It was a win-win for both of us.

Now, let's assess these styles in terms of their impact in negotiations using two criteria: 1. Nurturing relationships and 2. Devising solutions. The five styles we have described possess varying degrees of these two criteria. In the graph below, I present the styles in terms of the impact from low to high of two criteria on our negotiations.

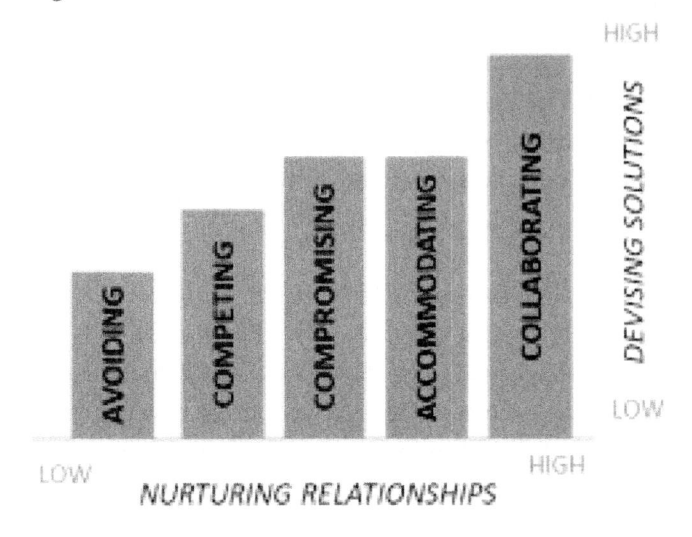

[Bar chart: AVOIDING, COMPETING, COMPROMISING, ACCOMMODATING, COLLABORATING bars increasing in height; y-axis DEVISING SOLUTIONS (LOW to HIGH); x-axis NURTURING RELATIONSHIPS (LOW to HIGH)]

The Avoiding style has a low impact both in terms of nurturing relationships and devising solutions, while the highest impact in devising solutions and nurturing relationships comes from the Collaborating style. The Compromising and Accommodating styles are both lower than Collaborating on devising solutions, but the Accommodating style ranks higher in nurturing relationships.

Summary

In this chapter, we discussed the key behaviors that are paramount to the success of negotiations. We started with a review of the demeanors that are essential to a negotiation and then studied the importance of understanding the other party's cultures and styles during the whole negotiation process from preparation to close. The checklist in Appendix B lists vital behavior considerations in a negotiation.

CHAPTER 7
Strategic Influencing Techniques

In the process of negotiation, influencing and persuading the other party to react in an anticipated manner becomes key to achieving desired outcomes.

Have you ever:
- wondered how to gain the attention and full focus from the other party?
- deliberated on how you could get a more favorable response or reception from them?
- wished that you could get valuable tips to influence somebody better?
- wondered how some people seem so adept at influencing people?

Answers to these questions lie in understanding and developing influencing skills. There are effective influencing techniques that, when applied, are expected to generate a specific behavior. As a result, such techniques can be used to elicit the anticipated response from the other party.

We use these techniques on a daily basis, yet most times we are unaware that we are using them. Also, since others might be applying these techniques in discussions with you, it is important to understand the effect these techniques are having on your negotiation. Most sales and marketing strategies apply one or more of these techniques. The techniques might not work in all situations. In some cases, more than one technique might be applied to get a desired result. Of the techniques used simultaneously, one might have a greater impact than the other. In this chapter, we will examine these techniques and the situations in which they might prove valuable. It is paramount that you understand these techniques and etch them in your head so they are second nature.

One of my favorite authors, Robert B. Cialdini, wrote about influence in his book *Influence: Science and Practice*. The book inspired me to delve deeper into the topic of negotiation and influence.

The techniques discussed in this chapter can be broken into three major categories: Connecting, Committing, and Controlling. Each of these categories comprises techniques that trigger a specific behavior. We will now review each of these three major categories. A trove of examples and stories will illustrate how these techniques are employed by negotiators. At the end of this chapter, a stimulating story highlights how several of these techniques are used by expert negotiators.

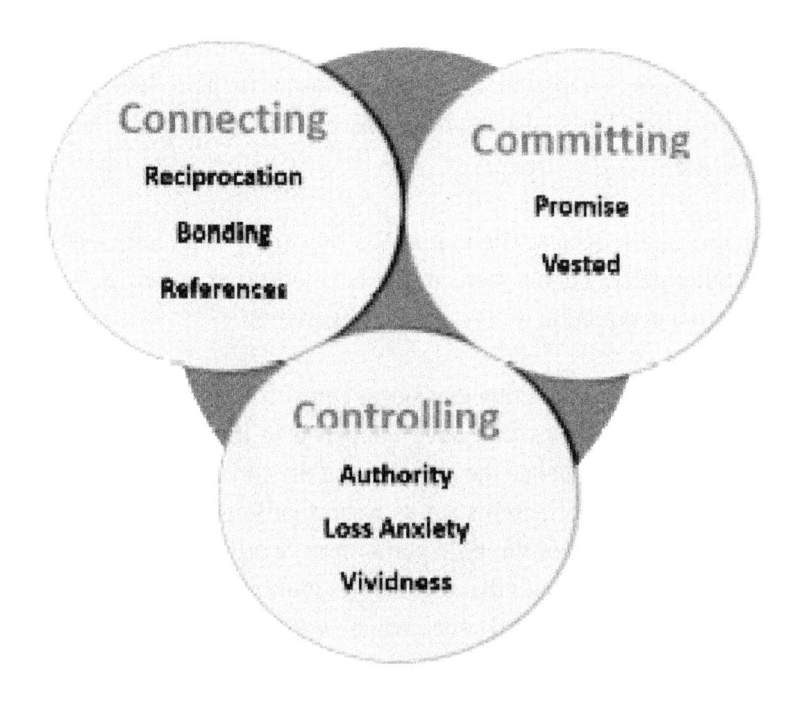

Connecting
Reciprocation
Bonding
References

Committing
Promise
Vested

Controlling
Authority
Loss Anxiety
Vividness

• • •

Connecting techniques

As the name suggests, these techniques are used to connect with the other party. The goal of these techniques is to develop a relationship that can be leveraged subsequently in influencing or in negotiations. In this category there are three distinct ways to make the connection: Reciprocation, Bonding, and References. Each of these techniques is important in its own right. However, these might even be combined in a negotiation. The effect of the techniques might vary depending on the situation.

Reciprocation

The common phrase "You scratch my back and I scratch yours" is a useful way to explain this technique. It is also commonly referred to as "give and take." Reciprocation is the act of returning in kind the receipt of helpful actions, favors, and generosity from the other.

It is a powerful technique to be used in influencing others. Accordingly, reciprocal acts can be used to gain leverage in negotiations. Let's discuss how this is done and their resulting benefits.

Reciprocation occurs when an action by a party is reciprocated by the other party. Such actions might have occurred in two ways: 1) prior to a negotiation or 2) during a negotiation.

First, let's discuss actions that occur prior to a negotiation. These are reciprocal actions that have happened in the past and can be called upon to influence the other during the current engagement in a negotiation. Prior actions act as a shortcut to get another person in a positive frame of mind. In some cases, a prior action can make an impact so significant that it generates multiple reciprocal actions thereafter. As we will see when we talk about Bonding, reciprocation that happens a few times over converts into a longer-term connection.

When I was younger, we used to receive *Reader's Digest* mailers regularly, and the package would contain stickers, calendars, and other useful items. I did not understand the concept of reciprocation at that time, but I can now relate to the technique used by *Reader's Digest*. The idea was to provide items to generate the future reciprocal action, namely to subscribe to the magazine.

Second, reciprocal actions as follows might occur during the current negotiation and can help in deriving a reciprocal behavior:
- Providing items or gifts;
- Favorable actions beneficial to the other party; and/or
- Providing accommodations or concessions

Reciprocation results not only from providing items or gifts but also from favorable actions. For example, being open and sharing information generates the anticipated behavior for the other party to share information.

Moreover, note that I mentioned "providing concession." This is important because even concessions are actions that would derive reciprocation. When a concession is provided, it results in a reciprocal action from the other party to also make concessions.

An example of reciprocation from day-to-day life comes to my mind in my recent negotiation with a colleague. She has strong experience in sales negotiation and has developed a course for sales professionals on contract negotiation. In order to tap into her knowledge, I asked her if she would spend an hour with me to present what she had developed. At the same time, we were working on a project for which she had a deadline to prepare a process flow diagram. She was struggling, because her team member was not available to prepare the process flow. As I had good experience in preparing flows, I offered to help her, and in return, she was able to spare some time for sharing her knowledge. Effective use of reciprocation!

Now, how do you apply reciprocation in your day-to-day life? This can be done in two ways:
1. Carry out any of the actions prior to the negotiation; and/or
2. Employ any of the actions stated above during your negotiation.

Next, assess if the actions are reciprocated. If required, subtly call upon the actions during the discussion. For example, in a recent discussion the other person remarked, "I hope the video I sent to you was exactly as you wanted!" This is a subtle way of highlighting the actions that derive reciprocation.

At the time of evaluating what influencing techniques can be applied to a negotiation, it is important to understand the power of reciprocation under different circumstances. Beware of a reciprocal action that is going to compel you to do something in exchange. Such an action might be a tactic that the other party is using. In this case, you will need to evaluate the reciprocal action and be ready to decline if required.

In some cultures, gift-giving might be customary and mandatory, so reciprocation occurs by default. However, in other scenarios when gift-giving is not customary, pay attention to the effect that the gift-giving can have on the negotiation. Furthermore, in some cultures this technique might not work since the power of reciprocation is not as strong. We discussed this in the previous chapter on behaviors and culture.

Bonding
The next under Connecting techniques is Bonding, a technique commonly employed by all of us. It refers to building relationships with all parties so that established bonds can be called up as a basis for influencing or gaining leverage in negotiations. Bonding is a powerful technique that brings an emotional touch and frequently triggers a specific behavior that is intended to ease the negotiation discussions. Forming the bond is an important prerequisite in most negotiations.

Bonding is often created by similarities, such as common habits, hobbies, place of origin, and associations. One peculiar experience showcases the importance of associations. In a previous role, my job responsibilities included developing and implementing policies. These policies would need to be reviewed with relevant stakeholders to get their feedback. One such stakeholder was known to be a tough partner. It was difficult to get him to agree, as he would always derail discussions. Having just learned this technique, I did some research and found that we went to the same business school. In my meeting with him, I brought up our association with the business school and talked about it for a few minutes. The discussion took a different turn once a connection was established. It became a lot easier to walk him through the policy and get acceptance.

We have often been part of conferences or seminars where one of the first agenda items is an icebreaker game. Often, the group activity is to introduce yourself and to find items common in the group. The goal of such an activity is to build relationships by sharing common hobbies, places, and associations.

Now, how does this technique work in your day-to-day life? The most common ways to enhance bonding are by gaining trust, nurturing a relationship, and demonstrating empathy.

- Gaining trust and demonstrating honesty results in win-win outcomes. In any situation, the moment trust is gained, a solid bond is established. Trust takes a long time to build but can be extremely powerful.
- Nurturing a relationship through constant contact over a period of time is another way to grow stronger bonds. We discussed previously that Reciprocation is powerful, as it creates the feeling of returning what was received. However, when reciprocation happens over and over again, it creates a long-term relationship and converts into bonding.
- Empathy refers to understanding and connecting with the feelings of another person. Demonstrating empathy and understanding the frame of mind of the other party is useful in improving bonding.
- Bonding can also be developed by helping others during times of urgency, crisis or uncertainty.

In recalling the story about Tom Perkins in Chapter 4 under the framing section, it was interesting in how he dealt with the external sales representative having just started his career at HP. It is also a relevant story about how Tom Perkins built credibility with the sales representatives. Credibility and trust are built gradually through a series of actions. He built trust by presenting himself as a helpful resource to the sales representatives in their interactions within HP. It was an effective technique that helped him to sail through the difficult position he was in.

One of my friends started a job at a new company in an executive role devising strategy for the company. Having previously worked in a fast-paced environment, it came as a surprise when he realized he had landed in a casual work environment. Even other executives casually urged him to take things easy. It took him some time to understand the operations and the people. He developed a grandiose vision for changes, but in gauging the people in the organization he thought it would be too drastic. So he conceived an interesting plan for his negotiation to implement the changes. His plan was to break his vision into multiple steps, like bite-sized chunks. It was like a game of chess taking small steps with the end result in mind. It would take multiple steps and would not be too much for the organization, but it would get the organization closer to his end vision. In this manner, he would build trust at every step and develop the bonding with the leadership team and other employees in the organization.

A successful negotiation is illustrated from the story of C. C. Myers, the president of the construction company C. C. Myers Inc. In January 1994, a massive earthquake of 6.6 on the Richter scale hit the Los Angeles area. It left behind destruction of the I-10 freeway, one of the busiest freeways in the world and a lifeline of the Los Angeles area. Traffic is typically bad even with the freeway in place, but it would be absolutely horrific without the freeway.

Estimates suggested a timeframe of 12 to 18 months to rebuild the freeway. The Office of Planning and Research estimated an economic loss of $1 million per day that the freeway was not operational. Myers, a building contractor with a reputation of rebuilding highways in quick time, was interested in this opportunity. He wanted to rebuild I-10. His negotiation to obtain this contract was not going to be easy. However, he was a skilled negotiator. He knew the clear rules of behaviors and techniques to arrive at a win-win negotiation.

Myers got a chance to meet the mayor and offer his help. At such a chaotic time, it is critical to frame the discussion very carefully. He highlighted the challenge presented by the crisis and offered to produce the solution in quick time. He particularly focused on empathy to create the bonding with the mayor.

In an effort to make it a win-win solution, he promised a six-month timeline for rebuilding the freeway and also signed up to pay a penalty of $200,000 for every day he was late. This was clearly framed as a positive for the mayor. Offers such as these provide the leverage for success in a negotiation. As per the CAV framework, this was clearly the value aspect that he built in the deal. The win-win solution benefited the city, the mayor, and the governor, in addition to Myers and his company. A skilled negotiator grabs all opportunities, so Myers negotiated for a bonus of $200,000 for every day the project was completed earlier than the assigned timeline. In the end, he won the contract with a 140-day timeline to complete the project. In fact, his team beat that target by 74 days, completing the whole project in just 66 days.

In many cultures where bonding is paramount, actual negotiations depend heavily on the network and relationships. The Chinese term *guanxi* emphasizes the importance of building relationships. Guanxi (pronounced as gwan-si) refers to the establishment of a relationship or connection with others. Hence, developing and maintaining guanxi becomes the primary component in the business environment. Guanxi is cultivated through regular interactions over a long period of time. As discussed earlier, reciprocation might be a one-time reciprocal exchange of offers and benefits. Multiple reciprocal exchanges of benefits and actions over a long period of time results in the development of a long-term relationship. Once established, guanxi can be leveraged whenever required in negotiations and can also be applied indirectly, i.e., when one person can use another person's guanxi with other people. This is termed as "guanxiwang," meaning a network of connections. Similarly, in many other cultures across the globe (such as Indian, Middle Eastern, and Latin American), building relationships is significant in closing deals. So, a global negotiator must be cognizant of the cultural impact of building relationships and incorporate this technique in their practice for the success of the negotiation.

References
The third technique under the Connecting category is References. In this world of ever-increasing options and growing content, references provide the social thumbs-up that allows making a decision a bit easier. The use of references is everywhere these days with the growing power of the Internet. We now live in a world that seems incomplete without the ecosystem of online referrals. Recommendations apply in travel, restaurants, entertainment, movies, jobs, and many more. Social marketing is now one of the primary methods of marketing.

Some very prominent examples of references are:
- Google search algorithm provides results based on a ranking derived from the number of page views, a unique form of online reference.
- Google maps and TripAdvisor reward users providing recommendations, a model based on social validation.

- Amazon's success is heavily based on reviews from shoppers or users.

References are equally valuable in negotiations. Often while negotiating, the use of references enhances the ability to effectively influence the other person.

The power of a reference can improve the chances for a successful negotiation. A great example is evident from the story of Google founders Larry Page and Sergey Brin as presented by David A. Vise and Mark Malseed in *The Google Story*. In early 1999, Page and Brin were looking for cash infusion for their internet search business and simultaneously approached venture firms Kleiner Perkins Caufield and Byers (KPCB) and Sequoia Capital. Stanford Professor David Cheriton provided a powerful reference in the negotiation that Page and Brin were having with venture capitalists John Doerr of KPCB, and Michael Moritz of Sequoia Capital. In order to persuade Doerr and Moritz further, Page and Brin also used their early angel investors, Ron Conway and Ram Shriram as their reference. Conway and Shriram extended the support that Page and Brin were looking for in their negotiation. These strong references enabled Page and Brin to land the funding that was the historic moment that propelled Google to the peak of the internet search business world.

As highlighted by Robert Cialdini, references are very powerful in the event of uncertainty. In a negotiation, when there is an element of uncertainty, the parties look to some kind of assurances that references are able to offer. Consider, for example, when a parent is negotiating with a child to go for a dental visit and is able to mention friends and other kids who have had an enjoyable dental visit.

So, how do you apply this technique in your day-to-day life? In the process of negotiating with a party, there are a couple of ways that references can be put into action:

1. Explore if any other parties can be brought to your aid as references. A good word put in by the references or a strong testimonial goes a long way. In one of my negotiation workshops, a participant of a consulting firm noted that he faced a big challenge in bringing a client to the table for negotiation. He was confident that once the client agreed to engage in the negotiation, his team would be able to convince the client of solutions they could deliver. In this case, I recommended utilizing references to play a key role in helping to bring clients to the table.
2. Highlight other people's experiences. Sharing how other people have benefited from what you are offering can serve as a reference to assist you in the negotiation.

• • •

Committing techniques

As the name suggests, these techniques are used to get the other party's commitment. The key while using these techniques is to get them onboard and agreeing to your point. By doing this, you can then generate a commitment that the other party will feel compelled to fulfill. This set of techniques comprises two different techniques that we all use frequently.

Promise

Negotiators frequently elicit a promise from the other party. The promise could be explicit or implicit. An explicit promise is provided in written form or verbally while an implicit promise could be made in the form of an action or a strong belief. The natural reaction of people is to fulfill promises. So they feel concerned if they made a promise they could not keep because the opposite party might call this out. In a negotiation, therefore, obtaining a promise helps in gaining compliance from the other party toward an objective. It is desirable to induce the promise early in the discussion.

Promises also have the ability to last for a long time. As an example, two parties entering into a partnership constitutes a promise that they are making to each other to fulfill the partnership. Such partnerships can be long lasting, and even when the partnership has to be renewed at some point in the future, the promise that was made originally can be called upon to reinforce the partnership.

In one of my workshops at a consulting firm, I brought up "Promise" as a technique, and a partner of the firm noted that he had used this technique a number of times with favorable results. He remarked that in his negotiations with a client he induced a commitment from the client executive to keep the error rate or number of adjustments at a specific low level. This leads the client to maintain this level. If the error rate or number of issues were to go beyond the agreed level, the partner would have to bring in more resources (a difficult task during peak season) and would therefore negotiate for an additional tier of fees. If the client succeeded in maintaining the specific level of error rates, it would be a win-win for both the client and the firm. The promise or commitment from the client executives weighed heavily on their minds and resulted in their best efforts to meet the commitment.

There are numerous examples in our daily life wherein promise is triggered to build a long-term relationship. Google frequently provides free storage or free OS to induce a user to be locked in for the future. In response to the benefits Google offers the user commits to continue using the services over the years. When negotiating with kids, we often use a combination of the techniques Promise and Reciprocation. We often hear parents saying, "If you do this, we will do this...is that a deal?" By confirming that it is a deal, the parents have given and received a promise.

How do you apply this technique in daily life?
In negotiations, it would be useful to obtain a promise from the other person, either prior to or during the negotiation. Once this promise is obtained, it is likely to be fulfilled. If and when required, call out the promise to get compliance.

Promises or commitments that are written, announced or shared with multiple people generate a stronger binding, and it is recommended to obtain a promise from the counterpart that is announced or shared widely. This is similar to the most common scenario we face in our corporate professional lives where one induces a commitment from a project partner to a deadline. The promise becomes even more effective when the deadline is announced widely, such as in a steering committee meeting.

One of my friends recounted a story about his move to the United States for work. The company executives made an announcement to his team that he was moving to Philadelphia even before his negotiation related to compensation and other benefits had concluded. We discussed that this was one way for them to get the promise from him on the move, but at the same time, the executives had explicitly promised to make their best efforts to help him with the move. This bode well for him too!

Then how does promise work in engaging with kids? My experience with a three-year-old kid demonstrates the impact of promise. We visited a friend who had two kids-a three-year-old and a seven-year-old. While it was easy to connect with the seven-year-old, it wasn't easy with the three-year-old who was anxious to meet new people. We tried the old trick that works with most kids-to get a high-five. It did not work. So we said she could give us a high-five after she had fun playing with our kids. This created a positive feeling in the way this information was presented, and she at least agreed to give us a high-five later. After a while, we checked back with her. I asked her for a high-five and again she was reluctant. At this time, I used the technique of promise. I made a questioning face and asked, "So, you did not have any fun and that is why you are not giving me a high-five?" Imagine this interaction of influencing a little kid. I asked her the question one more time, and this time she gave me a high-five. I asked her if she did have fun and she nodded shyly. Psychology shows that the promise did finally work with her.

Vested

This next technique under the Committing category is termed as "Vested." Based on my research and discussions with multiple people, this technique is one of the most commonly used tools for influencing. This technique is applicable when the principal objective is to get multiple parties onboard with an idea or a proposal. The most effective way is to convince the individual parties to "buy in" separately to the idea or proposal prior to the decision being announced or before voting on a proposal. This gives the parties a feeling of being vested in a decision. This is one way to foster collaboration, stimulate creativity and eventually generate an agreement.

Though the Vested technique is similar to Promise, the main difference is that promise can be with oneself or with another party; whereas, vested relates to discussions and reaching agreement with multiple parties in a negotiation.

In the United States, a process called *negotiated rulemaking* has been officially recognized since the establishment of the Negotiated Rulemaking Act in 1990. Negotiated rulemaking is a process used by federal agencies to develop a proposed rule in partnership with the interest groups affected by the rule. This process gives everyone who has a stake a chance to contribute towards the establishment of a rule before the agency proposes it in final form. Rules are therefore shared with smaller groups of stakeholders before they are launched. Vested is used similarly in negotiations.

In the corporate world, the use of the Vested technique is very common. Boardroom discussions frequently involve making a decision that needs a majority vote from the board members. Often the board member presenting an idea or proposal separately aligns with other board members on the direction in advance of the decision at a board meeting.

We also frequently use Vested in our professional world in project management and in policy-making. When we create or modify new policies or procedures, we align separately with all the key stakeholders who are affected by the proposals. The actual implementation or changes in the policies or procedures is facilitated by the prior consensus from the interested parties.

So, how do you apply this technique in daily life?

As a part of negotiations that involve multiple parties, discuss with the parties separately and individually to get them aligned. Once this is done successfully, the final result will be positive.

I read the Program on Negotiation case on Tommy Koh, 2014 winner of the Great Negotiator Award (established by Harvard's Program on Negotiation in 2000). It is a stimulating case that highlights the expert negotiation skills used by Tommy Koh and his team in the negotiation for the implementation of the United States and Singapore Free Trade Agreement ("USSFTA").

Multiple requests had accumulated from nations that wanted to enter into an FTA with the U.S., and the tiny country of Singapore was way down in the list. Singapore had ambitions of becoming the first Asian country to enter into an FTA with the U.S. Then Prime Minister of Singapore Goh Chok Tong agreed to propose the idea to President Clinton on USSFTA during a golf game in Brunei, and Clinton agreed for the FTA within twenty minutes after the game.

Tommy Koh was appointed as the chief negotiator to draft and execute the USSFTA on behalf of Singapore. Koh was a top negotiator, having previously had success with negotiations of the "Law of the Sea" and the Rio Earth Summit. He was the right man for the job. Koh, Ambassador Chan, and the team set about a multi-front negotiation. The team went about their preparation and engagement in a skillful way. They identified all the issues and areas to be presented in the negotiation.

From the facts presented in the case, it is evident that the Vested technique was the effective technique tool to apply in the circumstances. Koh's team conferred with 31 citizen advisory groups in the business community, 114 major companies, and a 59-strong caucus of representatives. They had 11 rounds of negotiations with multiple groups. This was still not the whole story. They also interacted with 353 congressmen and 78 senators in the process.

After all this great effort, when it was the final moment to vote on the FTA, it was approved by a majority of 272 out of 435 in the Congress and by 66 out of 100 in the Senate.

• • •

Controlling techniques
This final set of techniques is used to create an element of control over the other party. The goal of these techniques is to steer the other party towards an anticipated response. These techniques are:

authority, loss anxiety, and vividness. However, it is important to be aware of these techniques, as the other party might be equally adept at using these in negotiations. Let's now run through each of these controlling techniques.

Authority

We have all used "Authority" as a technique in many of our negotiations. It is the simplest and most intuitive technique to use. Imagine a mother trying to negotiate with a kid and the final resort for the mother is to mention the name of the father or vice versa.

How does Authority work and how can it be applied in daily life? Authority can be established based on facts, expertise, title or position, or rules or regulations. Influence of or information from a recognized authority can provide us with a valuable shortcut for deciding or persuading towards a desired course of action. Let's see how these are used to generate leverage.

- *Facts* can be used as an important source to add power in many cases where a decision is made on the basis of solid analyses based on data.
- *Expertise* is a powerful element to create an authority. An expert carries a higher reputation that people respect and follow.
- *Title or position* are based on the higher standing that induces the authority. Title or position is most often derived from a higher rank or wealth.
- *Rules and regulations* are considered a strong authority that people are compelled to follow.

Sachin Tendulkar, one of the world's best cricket players and certainly India's best for a long time, made an unusual request to the Board of Cricket in India. He was playing his 200th match and had decided it would be his last. He announced his retirement to the Board of Cricket and expressed his wish to allot the match to his home city, Mumbai. The Board reserves the right to make the decisions of the location of the matches and assigning it based on a player request is extremely rare. Multiple cities look for their chances to host matches, and there is a rotation schedule for locations to host matches. Mumbai would host the match "out of turn." In this case, the authority of position clearly applied, as Tendulkar had the reputation that the Board had to respect. The Board approved his request, and Mumbai was allotted the match as per Tendulkar's wish.

So how do we deal with situations where the other party uses authority? In some cases, we might not have an option. However, there are cases where you could satisfactorily respond to the use of authority.

One way to respond to the use of authority is to counter with authority. In our professional world, we frequently use authority. How often do we refer to the authority of an executive or a policy to gain leverage on projects? As an example, if one uses the authority of an executive, there is always the authority of another executive or a policy that can be brought in as a counter. Similarly, if one uses a policy as an authority, there is always an exception process that the policy owner can approve to bypass the guidance of the policy. It is vital, therefore, to use authority that cannot be easily dismissed. This authority could come from facts and data analyses that are not easy to ignore.

Another way is to arrive at innovative and creative solutions that will counter the effect of authority. Let's take an example to bring this to life. As we all know, when we talk about a class at school, there is little doubt that it is the professor who possesses the authority. Then how do you negotiate with the professor?

A real-life story comes from my MBA class on finance, one of the toughest subjects for most of the class. We were negotiating with the professor for a higher percentage allocation for class assignments and participation and lower for the final exam. Our objective was to reduce the percentage score assigned to the final exam to the lowest possible, and thereby reduce our stress. However, the professor stated that there was only so much he was allowed to do. He cited university rules, another level of authority by which he was governed.

Not getting much leeway in terms of the reduction in percentage allocation for the final exam, we asked the professor to consider an open-book final exam. The professor declined the request. Finally, one of my classmates came up with a creative idea. It was probably the last-ditch effort in the negotiation. He asked the professor if we could take group exams and looked around the class to get an affirmation of the idea. Taking his cue, a couple of other classmates chimed in with support for group exams. To the amazement and relief of everybody, our professor agreed with the idea. So, we took the exam in groups of three. At least three minds were better in attempting to tackle a difficult exam problem than taking the exam individually.

A colleague highlighted an example that brings the authority technique to the fore. Every month, she had to persuade several project managers in the technology organization to provide the required information for accounting and reporting. She had to negotiate the expected date and time that she would receive information since many of them did not adhere to the original timelines that she had stipulated. This is a common problem faced by professionals in the corporate world where they rely on information from another party. So, in order to make her work more efficient, she decided to use the Authority technique. She identified the key stakeholders who were impacted by this information and narrowed it down to the head of technology finance and the head of technology operations. The information from the project managers provided both these stakeholders key information for planning and monitoring technology projects, so she partnered with these key stakeholders to push down the message and drive the necessary behavior. This helped her implement a better process for the project managers to tender their information on a timely basis. Aligning with stakeholders with authority enabled her negotiation with the project managers to achieve her objective while also benefiting the key stakeholders.

Authority applies most notably in political negotiations. Common uses of authority in the political environment are the formation of a coalition or alliance of a few nations or the imposition of sanctions on any country by other countries. However, it is critical that authority is used carefully as it can backfire strongly.

As Authority is one of the easiest techniques available, it can be frequently employed by the other party. Awareness of situations where it is applied, assessment of the fairness and justified use, and preparation for ways to neutralize the effects becomes essential.

Loss Anxiety
This technique is as effective in sales and marketing as any other applicable techniques. We see this technique being routinely applied in the process of influencing the other party, as it triggers an immediate response due to the uneasiness caused by the element of loss. The sense of lost opportunity generates a specific human behavior to obtain or retain something. Competition is frequently used as a means to specify the loss anxiety.

Loss anxiety arises for three primary reasons:
- Availability - the feeling of something that will run out quickly due to quantity being scarce. Auctions for a rare item creates the availability loss through competition. Numerous items are sold as rare or collector's items that will not be available if that window of opportunity is missed.

- Urgency - the sense of limited time available to make a decision or perform an action. This technique calls for a quick, impulsive action when it is employed.
- Accessibility - the restrictions imposed on the use or access of something to a specified audience, thereby creating exclusivity. Accessibility is typically used to stipulate that the access or subscription is available only to specific members.

While I was yet unaware of this technique, I often reacted to the loss anxiety employed. It is a very common marketing strategy and is also effectively used in negotiations. In my first couple of interactions with the finance department at car dealers, I used to dread the negotiation on purchase of the extended warranty because the condition would be to purchase the warranty only at the time of signing the agreement and thereby causing loss anxiety. It is that uncertain time of buying a used car when one is not sure if the warranty will be useful, but a quick decision needs to be made. On one occasion I even bargained on the amount I would pay for the warranty. On another occasion I denied the additional warranty knowing that a comprehensive warranty for a full year was available and I would then shop for external warranties. Now that I am aware of this technique and teach negotiation, I advise participants not only to know how to use it but also to be on their guard for the application of the technique.

How do you apply this technique in daily life?

If there is any way to highlight that the other party will lose due to a delay in decision, it can be applied. Note, however, that this is a common technique and the other person might also apply it easily.

Have you watched the reality show *Shark Tank*? It is a gripping reality show on CNBC with several live examples of negotiation. I find it a good way to observe negotiation practices and influencing skills. While it is beneficial to follow the negotiation process that I have presented throughout this book, it is critical to analyze the use of techniques and behaviors.

In one of the episodes the participant, the owner of an innovative fishing line cutting tool, provided a great opening pitch with vividness (see the next technique). He threw the metal tools, told a story about the knife that almost cut off his toe, and cut several kinds of fishing lines using the new tool in front of the sharks. He also made one ring each for the sharks, based on a theme to derive reciprocation. He called Daymond John stylish and his most favorite shark.

His ask was for $120,000 for a 20 percent stake in his business. Mark Cuban and Robert Herjavec were the first two sharks to bow out. Then came the offer from Daymond, who proposed $120,000 for a 40 percent stake. The discussion moved on to Kevin O'Leary, who had just started questioning the participant when Daymond jumped in and asked, "Are you sure you want to go down the route with him? Because my offer may change after that." This was instant pressure. This is the classic example of loss anxiety—the loss of availability of the offer.

Soon, Kevin and Lori Greiner were also out, leaving just Daymond in the picture. At this time, what do you think the participant's position was? It was very weak indeed. He did not have any TRAIN, as only one shark was in the picture. The participant must surely have come with an idea of what percentage of his company he was actually willing to give away. His original offer was an anchor and Daymond cut that in half. The participant continued to negotiate in order to arrive at his goal of $120,000 for a 33 percent stake in his company. A weak TRAIN and loss anxiety that was created enabled Daymond to get more value out of the deal.

I wanted to specifically call out here that creating fear or threats or any other kind of pressure might be a tactic that works, but is not effective since it is likely to create distrust. In my opinion, these are hardball tactics to get an upper hand and are not valid forms of creating loss anxiety.

Vividness
Vividness is perhaps one of the most stimulating techniques used in negotiation. This technique refers to making the appearance of something much more vibrant or larger in proportion to influence the other party, resulting in an expected behavior. The idea is to make an immediate impact that creates a "wow" factor. Vividness comes from distinctive ideas, awe-inspiring videos, and other material, analogies, touching the heart, etc.

How does this technique work in daily negotiations?
Incorporating vividness as a technique can yield effective results. It leaves an impact on the mind that could drive the negotiation to successful results. So in any scenario, present it vividly such that it influences behavior and triggers a positive response.

Remember the car dealer negotiation experience that I shared in loss anxiety? The finance department is not only trained to use loss anxiety to its fullest, but they employ vividness too. In our experience with the car dealer the first time, the finance manager showed us a laminated picture of a broken-down car with service staff working on it on one side and an invoice for repairs worth thousands of dollars on the other side. A highly effective way to create the influence. And I must admit that it did.

Vividness can also come from simplicity. For Google, the vividness of a simple homepage captured attention owing to its minimalist effect. Being one of the most valuable properties on the Internet does not compel Google to reconsider its strategy. In our professional world, simplicity is extremely valuable. It is very effective when communicating a proposal to executives. We frequently need to present complicated processes and proposals to executives, and it is most effective to provide in a simple manner for easier decision-making.

Let's now look at a captivating story from Dee Hock's (founder and CEO Emeritus of Visa) book *Birth of the Chaordic Age* (first edition, 1999) and my analysis of the array of techniques used in negotiations in the process of the creation of Visa. Dee Hock learned immensely from his seniors and used the techniques masterfully. Here's the story:

Bank of America had pioneered the bank card business with their BankAmericard. They created the licensing structure and built a strong licensee base. They had high volumes but also had operational issues. In the early 1970s, a new organization, National BankAmericard Incorporated (NBI) was formed, and the proposed model stipulated the licensees to surrender their BankAmericard licenses and transfer membership to the newly formed NBI. The process of creating this new organization was complicated, as there were thousands of licensees who had to be brought under the umbrella of the new organization.

Dee Hock worked very hard to get the agreement from the licensee banks to join the new organization. His boss at National Bank of Commerce advised him that it was critical to reach the senior executives or the members of the board who make such decisions at those organizations. So, it would be a better negotiation if they managed to persuade industry senior leaders to align with their idea and to seek their help in influencing other industry leaders. This depicts the influencing skills **Vested** and **References**. The young Hock reached out to Sam Stewart, the vice chairman of the Board of Bank of America, with whom he had already created a bonding by gaining his trust while proposing the idea of the formation of NBI. Stewart and Hock reached out to influential CEOs who were inducted as part of the Executive Officers' Organizing Committee (EOOC). Bringing members of the EOOC onboard with the idea was a major step toward the objective of signing up more licensee members. EOOC members were requested to schedule meetings with other licensee banks in their region and highlight their effort and commitment. As banks started committing to the new organization, they were requested to talk to banks that were hesitant or unsure. This brings the **References** technique to life. Some banks remained uncommitted while some were opposed to the idea. It was important to know more about the individuals making a decision and understand their interests to guide them to the end result.

It was understood that if two-thirds of the banks committed to the formation of NBI, it would be sufficient to meet the required numbers. The banks which did not commit to the formation of the new organization had the option to join any time after the initial period, but specific privileges, including voting or serving on the board, would not be available. It was also pertinent to note that there would be no new licensing by Bank of America. At one stage, there was only one licensee bank that had not agreed. It was important for Hock to call it out, and so he talked to the senior executive of the bank. He specified with intent to the executive that all other licensee card-issuing banks had signed up to join the new organization. The officer immediately got the important message. Not surprisingly, the executive firmly replied, "Count us in!" Hock had made effective use of **Loss anxiety** as a means of winning over banks that did not join the group. Finally, the technique **Vividness** was applied when the whole concept was presented to all the licensees. The unique concept of the new organization, along with the rights and obligations as owner-members, was revolutionary. All these factors proved critical in the final outcome of the successful formation of NBI in the United States.

The real negotiation started when international licensees wanted to jump on the bandwagon of NBI's success. However, that was not going to be an easy task to accomplish as there were a multitude of criteria that presented big hurdles, such as differences in the names of the card, marketing, legal systems, computer systems, and operations. This was compounded by a variety of languages, currencies, and cultures. Dee Hock was appointed to take this initiative forward. In a meeting of the international licensees in Mexico to establish an international organization, there were multiple differences and signs of breach of trust. This was concerning! In a negotiation, trust and bonding are the primary criteria to enable the negotiation to move forward smoothly. At the follow-up meeting in Spain, Hock pressed his concerns around trust to Ken Larkin, one of the senior members of Bank of America, urging him to intervene and announce full commitment from Bank of America. In that meeting, Larkin announced Bank of America's support for the establishment of the international organization. This was the significant reference that provided a positive push to the discussion. All licensee banks agreed to move forward with the discussions.

Nonetheless, some disagreements and conflicts among the licensees lingered. Licensees remained true to their positions instead of the larger interests. No matter, Hock remained optimistic. In his book he noted how, at critical moments, all participants felt compelled to succeed and had been willing to compromise. Winning or losing aside, a larger sense of purpose and concept of community seemed to be paramount.

Hock and some of the other committee members got together to come up with a phrase that would represent what the group was feeling. They devised the expression "The will to succeed, the grace to compromise" which was translated in Latin to *Studium ad prosperandum, voluntas in conveniendum.* They then contacted a local jeweler to create sets of cufflinks for each member of the committee. Each cufflink would be decorated with half of the Earth and either the phrase *Studium ad prosperandum*" or "*Voluntas in conveniendum.* The cufflinks were to be presented to committee members. At a meeting in San Francisco, which was the last chance to resolve the conflicts among the licensees, things did not start out well. The disagreements could not be resolved. At one stage. there was a strong indication that the meeting would end abruptly and the effort would have to be abandoned.

That evening members were invited to dinner at a fine French restaurant. At the dinner tables that night, the members were presented their cufflink gifts. Hock mentioned that the gifts were a remembrance of the efforts for the rest of their lives. These gifts grabbed the attention of all the members when they examined the contents of the box and left a lasting impression. He asked them to wear the cufflinks to the meeting on the next day, noting that they would either serve as a reminder of how they failed to unite the world or how they were able to come together in the spirit of success and compromise. This was a great idea, one which helped build trust. Furthermore, the idea helped everybody understand and appreciate that they were in this together. The next morning was a different day. Members had worked hard overnight talking to executives at their banks to come to a consensus. The power of reciprocation and promise was strong. While members were compelled to reciprocate the gesture from Hock, there was an evident promise to reach a compromise, since all members had worn the cufflinks and were determined to work out a deal. Positions had been discarded and agreement was quickly reached.

Summary
We have reached the end of the journey through the assortment of valuable techniques. Techniques are proven to be extremely effective at influencing the other party. After all, we are dealing with people, and it is human behavior to be influenced by these techniques. However, as stated at the beginning of this chapter, it is important to note that not all techniques work in all circumstances. In some cases, multiple techniques can be employed, but some might not result in any benefit. In Appendix

A, I have presented an assessment of influencing skills. I encourage you to complete the exercise to assess your influencing abilities and use the analysis of the assessment that can act as a guide for areas of improvement.

CHAPTER 8
My Negotiation Journey

My journey in the world of negotiation began with a study of influence and negotiation practices as a part of my MBA program. In our leadership course in 2014, we were introduced to *Influence: Science and Practice*, by Robert Cialdini, a book that illustrates influencing behaviors using stimulating examples and real case studies and opening the mind to further exploration of the subject. Interest in learning more on the topic and developing my understanding further led to reading several articles and watching videos on influence. It is interesting how several techniques are so often subtly used for influencing and become a reflex for future actions. I delved deeper into this topic and developed a structural approach to influencing techniques presented in this book.

The next experience that opened my eyes to negotiation practices was from the course on negotiation behaviors in February 2015. As a part of the course, we were introduced to *Getting to Yes* by Prof. Roger Fisher, Prof. William Ury, and Prof. Bruce Patton, and *Negotiating Rationally* by Prof. Max Bazerman and Prof. Margaret Neale. In addition, we were provided several opportunities to negotiate and apply strategies via multiple simulation exercises, which highlighted several important areas related to different types of negotiations. From casual chats during and after class, I gathered the key aspects and practices that apply to every situation, whether it is a simple two-party negotiation or a complex multi-party negotiation. My MBA program ended over the next few months, but attraction to the topic continued to grow. Within a short time after graduating, I had finished reading *Getting to Yes* and *Negotiating Rationally*, and added *Bargaining for Advantage*, by G. Richard Shell, to my reading log.

During this time, I had some discussions with my colleagues at work and agreed to share some of the relevant learnings that would benefit everybody in the team. After a lot of research and reading, I put together a short presentation on influencing techniques and negotiation skills, and shared it with my team in Singapore in February 2016. This was my first experience in presenting on the topic of negotiation and the feedback from the session was motivating. I immediately started working on enhancing the content.

At the same time, I joined the Harvard Law School's Program on Negotiation to dive deeper into the fascinating world of negotiations. The wealth of information available on the website of Program on Negotiation and the trove of simulation cases are valuable sources for anybody who wishes to enhance their knowledge base in negotiations.

In May 2016, I expanded my negotiation presentation to a half day course on *Negotiation Concepts and Techniques* and included a negotiation simulation. This was Module 1 of my negotiation workshop. I started enjoying this newly developed passion of hosting workshops and was now ready to explore presenting my workshops outside the audience in my organization. This opportunity came my way in June 2016 when I was invited to host a couple of workshops for over 40 sales and operations staff at a

U.S. multinational company and the sessions generated positive feedback. This was a great development in this journey.

Between May 2017 to October 2017, I started hosting negotiations at work in the United States. At the same time, around September 2017, I commenced further expansion of the course to develop Module 2 on behaviors. In October 2017 I completed the certificate program on negotiation at Harvard Law School and it was a great experience to meet some of the esteemed professors.

The belief in the direction I had taken was further strengthened after attending the certification program. I was motivated to continue my research on the topic. From December 2017 to March 2018, I hosted multiple workshops in different locations. Every workshop was an opportunity to learn from the participants' perspectives. Around this time, I had discussions with my brother focused on building my passion. It was a valuable conversation for me, as he suggested that I could demonstrate the passion for the subject by writing a book. I interviewed some people on their negotiation experiences, recollected my own experiences, and read several books to build stories for this book.

In May 2018 I was ready with my Module 2 of negotiation focusing on Key Behaviors. Some of the key discussions in this module relate to the impact of culture and individual styles on our negotiations. This topic generated heavy interest from participants. September 2018 marked another first, as I combined both modules into a full-day workshop at a Big 4 consulting firm. The session was well-received and requests poured in for additional sessions. Shortly afterwards, a couple of friends or colleagues stated that they would like to consult me for their experiences and get advice on how to deal with the situations. The workshops continued in 2019 across different locations but primary focus shifted towards launching this book. In 2019, I also published the original edition of this book and received great reviews and feedback. It received an Amazon best-seller rank.

2020 was a milestone year. While the world was reeling under the impact of COVID, I realized opportunities and developed my interests further. I was invited to join several podcast shows or live events as a speaker. I also started hosting remote workshops. Later in 2020, I launched my second book, *We Can Negotiate Too!*, for children and young adults to learn negotiation early in life. The book was ranked #1 in new releases on Amazon and was well received across the reading community and appreciated by children and youth. This provided the platform for me to start teaching children the essential negotiation skills. In 2021, I launched my venture **_Propelurs Consulting_** to further my passion of teaching negotiation and other super skills to a wide audience. In 2022, I successfully completed a full year of teaching negotiation at two schools in Chennai with great review and feedback. Teaching, content writing and speaking became my primary focus and I dedicated my full time to it.

Friends, colleagues, and professionals frequently ask what my ROI from the MBA program was. My clear answer is that the passion for negotiations is a direct ROI from an MBA. The passion was generated from the courses on influence and negotiation behaviors, and I worked hard on growing my passion. The story of the Chinese bamboo plant comes to mind. Once the bamboo is planted from seed, it needs to be provided water and fertilizer for five years before the shoots start appearing. Once the shoots appear, the plant can grow to a height of 90 feet in just six weeks. I believe I have been nurturing my passion since 2016 and will continue to do so until I see the "shoots" arise and reach lofty heights.

REFERENCES

Books and studies

Bazerman, Max and Neale, Margaret A. (1992). *Negotiating Rationally.*

Cialdini, Robert. *(2014, Fifth Edition). Influence Science and Practice.*

Fisher, Roger, Ury, William and Patton, Bruce. (2011 Third Edition). *Getting to Yes.*

Hock, Dee. (1999). *Birth of the Chaordic Age.*

Perkins, Thomas J. (2007). *The Valley Boy.*

Polly, Matthew. (2018) *Bruce Lee: A Life.*

Shell, G. Richard (2006, Second Edition). *Bargaining for Advantage.*

Sorkin, Andrew Ross (2010). *Too Big to Fail.*

Tendulkar, Sachin with Majumdar, Boria (2014). *Playing It My Way.*

Vise, David A., and Malseed, M. (2005). *The Google Story.*

House, R. J., Hanges, P. J., Javidan, M, Dorfman, P. W. and Gupta, V. (2004). *Cultures, Leadership and Organizations: A 62 Nation GLOBE Study.*

Web

Chapter 3: Amazon VAT
City A.M., April 6, 2018 "Amazon and Ebay to share data with HMRC in bid to tackle overseas tax evasion"
Sky News, October 24, 2017 "HMRC accused of blatant hypocrisy after signing deal with amazon"

Chapter 3: Microsoft and Google
Neowin, February 11, 2016 "Microsoft apps now preloaded on 74 android OEMs"
Geekwire, September 30, 2015 "Microsoft and Google reach sweeping settlement in longstanding patent suits)
Microsoft, February 10, 2016 "Microsoft services are available on more devices than ever before through agreements with device partners"

SeekingAlpha, October 1, 2015 "Microsoft sacrificing android patents licensing favor platform agnostic growth"

Chapter 3: Ikea story
East Bay Times, November 14, 2018 "Unique Ikea Store coming to Dublin"
The Independent, November 15, 2018 "Dublin Approves IKEA Store and Walkable Shopping"
SFGate, November 14, 2018 "New IKEA coming to Bay Area, but it will look different from other stores"

Chapter 3: Roosevelt story
CNBC, Aug 5, 2008 "Becoming a Negotiation Genius" by Deepak Malhotra and Max Bazerman

ACKNOWLEDGEMENTS

Having grown up with books all around the house, I always wondered whether I would ever have a book with my name as the author. My mother, Dr. Neela Jagannathan, and father, Professor V. R. Jagannathan, are both successful authors. I feel proud to have them as a source of inspiration and continuous support towards the accomplishment of this dream.

A big motivation in my life has come from my wife, Jyothi. The support and encouragement from her has been overflowing and helps me to keep going. She has been my partner in many negotiations, and we have learned from several experiences together. The support and regular check in from both my daughters, Shreya and Nithya, has provided the drive. The excitement around the house when we looked at cover designs spoke for itself. My brother, Pramit, renders sound advice whenever I reach out to him. He was the first to say, "You should write a book if you are passionate about this."

A special note of thanks to the editor of this book, Gary Klinga. Here's what he had to say about the book from his detailed review:

"*Negotiation Quotient* offers the reader practical teachings to build confidence and control in any situation as a negotiator. The author shares valuable nuggets of information in a clear and positive tone, elaborating on key points with many interesting case studies. This guide is a must for anyone who wants to attain the power and skills needed to win as a negotiator. If you are serious in becoming a powerful negotiator, then here's a golden chance to set you on the right course toward success. Anuj Jagannathan has unquestionably arrived on the scene as the new mentor of the craft of negotiation."

Friends, colleagues, and family helped read parts of the book. Some friends and colleagues also shared their experiences that converted into examples and cases for the book.

APPENDIX A
Influencing Skills Assessment

INSTRUCTIONS

The objective of this exercise is to assess your influencing abilities.

There are 20 statements below that commonly apply to everybody. For each statement, provide a rating from 1 (Never), 2 (Occasionally), 3 (Neutral), 4 (Mostly) to 5 (Always) based on how accurately the statement applies to your behavior in real situations.

RATING

Statement	Rating
1. I consider all the influencing techniques that apply during the preparation phase and plan to use them effectively.	
2. I analyze the other party's words and actions to assess their influencing abilities.	
3. I evaluate the impact of cultures in the process of influencing others.	
4. In a negotiation, I highlight how the other party will benefit from the agreement.	
5. While engaging with the other party, I provide benefits I can easily provide, even if not specifically asked for.	
6. In negotiations involving multiple parties, I prepare in advance by engaging the parties offline and highlighting benefits for them.	
7. In a negotiation, I highlight the unique aspects of my proposal points that others cannot match.	
8. I build trust in my audience by actively listening and understanding their perspectives.	
9. I pack a punch in my points by using strong criteria such as facts, numbers or data analysis.	
10. If the other party provides a concession, I remember and reciprocate the gesture.	
11. I go out of the way to help others in an effort to build a liking and credibility, nurturing a relationship for the long term.	

12. I provide strong support to my viewpoints using highly relevant and credible sources.	
13. If I know that the information I have is unique, I highlight the value lost to the other party if the information is no longer available.	
14. I impress upon the other party that my view aligns with common practice or social trends.	
15. I engage references or mediators to build the connection with the other party and provide them more confidence.	
16. I carefully bring out the associations or similarities I share with other party to develop bonding.	
17. I highlight to the other party that they had previously committed to a specific point in discussion.	
18. I use vivid methods of framing and presenting data in order to generate positive interest and agreement.	
19. I make presentations lively by using vivid analogies, examples and descriptions.	
20. I strive to understand all the parties in a multi-party negotiation and align with each one of them separately on interests.	
Total Rating	

Refer to the table below to review your rating.

>70 **Super Influencer**	Congratulations! Your ability to influence ranks among the best.
60-69 **Among The Better**	Awesome! Your influencing skills impress in many areas but would benefit from polishing some aspects.
40–59 **Getting There**	Practice makes you better. Focus on some areas you need to develop and you will get to the top.
<40 **Need to practice**	Buck up! Study some of the influencing skills and build them into your day-to-day practice.

INFLUENCING SKILLS ASSESSMENT - EXPLANATION

Statement	Technique
1. I consider all the influencing techniques that apply during the preparation phase and plan to use them effectively.	GENERAL
2. I analyze the other party's words and actions to assess their influencing abilities.	GENERAL
3. I evaluate the impact of cultures in the process of influencing others.	GENERAL
4. In a negotiation, I highlight how the other party will benefit from the agreement.	BONDING
5. While engaging with the other party, I provide benefits I can easily provide, even if not specifically asked for.	RECIPROCATION
6. In negotiations involving multiple parties, I prepare in advance by engaging the parties offline and highlighting benefits for them.	VESTED
7. In a negotiation, I highlight the unique aspects of my proposal points that others cannot match.	LOSS ANXIETY
8. I build trust in my audience by actively listening and understanding their perspectives.	BONDING

9. I pack a punch in my points by using strong criteria such as facts, numbers or data analysis.	AUTHORITY
10. If the other party provides a concession, I remember and reciprocate the gesture.	RECIPROCATION
11. I go out of the way to help others in an effort to build a liking and credibility, nurturing a relationship for the long term.	BONDING
12. I provide strong support to my viewpoints using highly relevant and credible sources.	AUTHORITY
13. If I know that the information I have is unique, I highlight the value lost to the other party if the information is no longer available.	LOSS ANXIETY
14. I impress upon the other party that my view aligns with common practice or social trends.	REFERENCES
15. I engage references or mediators to build the connection with the other party and provide them more confidence.	REFERENCES
16. I carefully bring out the associations or similarities I share with other party to develop bonding.	BONDING

17. I highlight to the other party that they had previously committed to a specific point in discussion.	PROMISE
18. I use vivid methods of framing and presenting data in order to generate positive interest and agreement.	VIVIDNESS
19. I make presentations lively by using vivid analogies, examples and descriptions.	VIVIDNESS
20. I strive to understand all the parties in a multi-party negotiation and align with each one of them separately on interests.	VESTED

APPENDIX B
Checklist for Negotiation Process*

General

☐ Evaluate the impact of cultures right through the process
☐ Know your style and constraints, and evaluate the impact on negotiations
☐ Determine the method of engaging: In-person or remote?

Prepare

☐ Determine what approach is applicable: Distributive or Integrative
☐ Devise your own CAV Framework analysis
☐ List your own interests
☐ Assess interests of the other party, and find mutually beneficial solutions
☐ List your alternatives and determine TRAIN
☐ Gauge what the other party's alternatives are
☐ Determine who is the other party's key decision-maker, and note the leader culture
☐ Learn about style of the key decision-maker to customize strategies accordingly

- ☐ Study the national culture / society culture, and note the nuances of the cultures
- ☐ Understand the organizational culture, if applicable
- ☐ Assess techniques that apply, and which technique might work best in the situation
    - ☐ Reciprocation - Are there reciprocation actions that you can call upon to influence?
    - ☐ Bonding - Can bonding help you to derive better solutions?
    - ☐ References - Identify references you can leverage during negotiations.
    - ☐ Promise - Are you able to leverage a promise to influence?
    - ☐ Vested - Incorporate this technique when dealing with multiple stakeholders.
    - ☐ Authority - Assess the use of authority by either party; find ways to respond to the authority.
    - ☐ Loss Anxiety - Evaluate the impact of loss anxiety in the negotiation.
    - ☐ Vividness - Identify ways to present information to make a strong, lasting impact.
    - ☐ Ascertain all the requirements to a successful closure of the negotiation, such as approvals or communication; pay attention to regulatory requirements
    - ☐ Prepare for your anchor with justifiable criteria
- ☐ Determine any potential conflict matters, and prepare solutions to resolve

Engage

- ☐ Build on your interests and theirs through the engagement
- ☐ Determine interests of key decision-maker and develop solutions accordingly
- ☐ Revisit your list of alternatives; confirm other party's alternatives
- ☐ Execute appropriate framing methods in your engagement
- ☐ Ensure anchors are properly delivered, and carefully handled during the engagement
- ☐ Identify any additional stakeholders that need to be informed or need to approve
- ☐ Ensure that the approvers and signatories are available at close
- ☐ Ensure you earn respect at the table and build trust; demonstrate empathy
- ☐ Use communication essentials
- ☐ Demonstrate confidence and appropriate body language; assess these aspects of the other party to adapt to their behavior
- ☐ Apply techniques assessed during preparation that might work in the situation
- ☐ Decide the level of information exchange based on interactions
- ☐ Walk into the negotiation with optimism (negoptimism)
- ☐ Adapt your style according to the situation, as applicable

Close

- ☐ Complete the agreement on all points
- ☐ Communicate agreement to all relevant parties
- ☐ Determine and agree on the terms of contract
- ☐ Ensure all approvals and sign offs are obtained
- ☐ Ensure post-signing formalities of communication are complete

*Refer to chapters for details on all the checklist points

PROPELURS *presents*

NEGOTIATION ARENA

AN INNOVATIVE, INTERACTIVE AND INTERESTING PLATFORM TO LEARN NEGOTIATION.

WWW.NEGOTIATION-ARENA.COM

WWW.PROPELURS.COM/NEGOTIATION-ARENA

INFO@PROPELURS.NET
+91 6380060041

Ideated, designed and developed by
Anuj Jagannathan

Printed in Great Britain
by Amazon